the Way

God's Call on an Ordinary Family to His Extraordinary Life

Amy Boykin

The Way: God's Call on an Ordinary Family to His Extraordinary Life

Amy R. Boykin, ©2019 All Rights Reserved

www.wayministries.org

Ultimate design, content, editorial accuracy and views expressed or implied in this work are those of the author.

Cover and Book Design by William E.G. Johnson Design | Illustration. More brilliant illustrations at garrisonthestronghold.com

Names and details in some anecdotes and stories have been changed to protect the identities of persons involved.

Feel free to quote up to 200 words in print or online with full attribution to the book. For longer quotations or multiple quotations, contact Amy boykin.amy@gmail.com

ISBN 978-0-578-48042-8 (Paperback)

This book is dedicated to my Lord and Savior, Jesus Christ

*Jesus answered, "I am the way and the truth and the
life. No one comes to the Father except through me."*

John 14:6

Table of Contents

PREFACE

In 2006 my husband Michael and I were living the American Dream. Successful in our real estate business, we had built our life around many accolades and accomplishments. I considered myself a successful Christian as well, but I yearned for something more. I didn't know what that 'more' looked like, but I fervently sought God for an answer. Quite unexpectedly, God answered by telling me and Michael to move our family of 6 from Austin, Texas, to the Bahamas.

Our children were very young at the time: son James was 3, daughters Josie and Marley were 5 and 7 respectively and Luke, the eldest, was only 8. How were we supposed to make a move like that happen? How were we to work and live? God remained silent and with no other details or answers given, we waited.

This uncertainty became the catalyst for God to see if I would step out in faith and trust Him completely, whether He provided those directives or not. As I dragged my feet through the agony of waiting, God began a painful purification process. It was that refinement that brought me to a state of obedience and preparedness. I was now fully ready to surrender everything to God and leave my comfortable Texas life to heed His beckoning.

Fast forward to August of 2010 when my family and I arrived on a tiny island off Eleuthera in the Bahamas. 'Eleuthera' is the Greek word for *freedom*, which God began to reveal in my life one challenge at a time. Through miracles, difficulties and blessings, God's sovereignty reigned as I was now on the narrow road of God's Love. This new journey in me had affects that rippled out to my children, my husband and countless others as the Holy Spirit taught me to live completely relying on Him and the Word of God.

The Way is a story of that journey.

Although I initially wrote this book in 2016 and today have spiritually matured beyond what I have written in this memoir, God implored me to share my family's journey so you, Beloved, may experience and ultimately desire the abundant life Jesus speaks about. I found abiding in Jesus truly is loving God and naturally results in loving your neighbor. This life of obedience by faith is Jesus' Way of living and bears His fruit for His kingdom expansion. By His amazing Grace, Jesus desires all to follow Him. When you do this, Beloved, you live in His freedom resulting in His fullness. This is truly the life Jesus speaks about in John 10:10 when He says, "I came that they may have life and have it abundantly." This call is for all believers and not restricted to a one-time event but unfolds daily as my family and I have found, even beyond what I have written about in these pages. My hope is you, Beloved, will conform to a lifestyle of this intimacy and sense God's joy as you experience the overflowing life of Jesus' love.

By Faith In Jesus,

Amy Boykin
Destin, Florida

Fall 2018

SECTION ONE

FAITH

And he said to all, "If anyone would come after me, let him deny himself and take up his cross and follow me. For whoever would save his life will lose it, but whoever loses his life for my sake will save it. For what does it profit a man if he gains the whole world and loses or forfeits himself?"

Luke 9:23–25

Introduction

Invitation to the Feast

Behold, I stand at the door and knock. If anyone hears my voice and opens the door, I will come in to him and eat with him, and he with me.

Revelation 3:20

Less than twenty-four hours before I would board our plane to the Bahamas I anxiously said to my sister-in-law on our morning run, "Angie, I really don't know if I can do this. I really don't."

The inward turmoil I was undergoing had kept me awake for many sleepless nights and finally I gave voice to my anxious heart. I noticed the concern in her eyes; it seemed like she might really understand the weight of all the circumstances that had led me to this painfully pivotal decision. But she responded otherwise.

"Oh, Amy I am sure it will be okay, and even if it is not you can always come back."

This is exactly the worldly perspective I had been struggling with the last few years. As we neared the last turn towards the bridge, I realized I must stand firm in my decision. *No Lord, Angie is wrong. That thinking is what I have told myself for years now and I must follow through. I know this move is much more than I can ever imagine.*

On that hot August morning, God used my sister-in-law's words to give me an ultimatum: *Your way, Amy? Or Mine?*

The road was clear in my head. I saw two paths. One resembled what I had already experienced for much of my life: abundance and prestige all stemming from my hard-working efforts to succeed and accomplish it all. The other path was vague and cloudy, filled with doubt and the unknown. All my husband and I heard was the Holy Spirit summoning us to move to the Bahamas. That was it.

There were no signs, no details about where to live, what to do for work or where our four children would attend school. *How will we survive?* Michael and I would ask God in our prayer time. But silence ensued. As we pondered whether we'd heard this call right, we would ask, *Are we making this up, God?*

Yet no answers came. Unbeknownst to me, God in His mysterious way was answering the very prayer I had prayed so fervently the year before.

It was 2005 and in that year I joyfully had my third child. From an outsider's perspective, my life looked picturesque, filled with all the trappings of the American dream. But inwardly I had questioned God, *Is this it, Lord?* It seemed like there was more to life, but I was uncertain what "more" I wanted. God in His faithfulness led me to a book that encouraged readers to pray the words of 1 Chronicles 4:10 every morning. For three months I personalized this and diligently prayed for my family and myself, "Oh Lord that you would bless me and my family indeed and enlarge our territory, and that your hand might be with us, and that you would keep us from harm so that it might not bring us pain!"

I had full confidence because I was a "good Christian woman" God would also do for me and my family as He had done for Jabez, the man who prayed this prayer. The next line reads, "And God granted what he asked." At this point, I had no idea that the "blessing" I thought I was asking for was not what I had been taught my entire life. I had been raised believing God's favor was similar to the world's idea of favor. The concept that more prosperity, more success, more respect, more of anything and everything equated fulfillment; that meant "blessing" to me.

God in His infinite wisdom was about to reveal that His idea of blessing was to be rooted and established in His character working through me to accomplish His desired outcome. It did not look like the world or anything of the world. Being blessed was not a dream of more of anything but Jesus alone. Learning this foundational truth would require sacrifice and faith that I did not yet have but that God would supply.

God had planted a growing discontent, an inward gnawing of something lacking in my life, the insatiable desire leading me to this thought. Just like God answered Jabez, he answered me one year later in 2006 with a command that required a choice: His will or mine? This answer was in the call to move to the Bahamas; my family and I were being called to the Great Feast. Jesus' invitation for my family recalled the words in Luke 14:16–17, "But he (Jesus) said to him, "A man once gave a great banquet and invited many. And at the time for the banquet, he sent his servant to say to those who had been invited, 'Come for everything is now ready.'" Jesus was telling me to trust Him, to 'Come' to Him just like He told the invited guests. Luke records one of Jesus' disciples saying, "Blessed is everyone who will eat bread in the kingdom of God!"

Neither Michael nor I understood the meaning behind this statement of a believer's life being "blessed" by coming to God's feast. In the original

12

language, the word "blessed" describes a follower of Jesus' enviable position from God's favor. This merit can only be received by grace in obedience to Jesus Christ through faith. Jesus was calling me and Michael to a life of feasting on Christ alone by our actions aligning with our words. Attending his dinner party would be evidence of our allegiance to His call. Jesus was to be the bread of our life. Our nutrients, our sustenance, our very existence was to be on the gospel of grace that only He supplies.

Although we'd heard the invitation, "Come to the Bahamas," our responses were like those people recorded further in Luke 14, verse 18, "But they all alike began to make excuses." We also began to list excuses as to why we could not come join Him in the feast that he had for us in the Bahamas. We didn't recognize this was the only celebration that would provide the abundant life Jesus speaks about in John 10:10, "...I came that they may have life and have it abundantly."

* * * * *

As I hugged Angie goodbye on that warm August morning in 2010, I knew the course of my eternity hinged on full surrender to what God had asked Michael and I to do four years prior. Although our family had no support from anyone to move forward with this change of course in life, this only heightened the sense of urgency to proceed with our decision. As I got back into my SUV that morning, I pondered the questions that continued to swirl, *Would I believe God? Could I trust Him? Did I love Him? Would I really allow God to be the Master of my life? Would I come to the 'Great Banquet'?*

For the thousandth time, I began to replay the story of events that led me to this crucial time in my life. Double-mindedness persisted and I decided rehashing the details of how Michael and I had arrived at abandoning a lifetime of dreams would give me confidence or clarity that I had not yet obtained. Could remembering change my mind? Or would I trust my decision and obey God? Was it the lack of approval for confirmation from anyone that was driving me crazy? Finally, I succumbed to anxiety and dropped my head back on the seat rest while my fists clenched to the bottom of my steering wheel. Staring at the pale green water of Lady Bird Lake I watched the boats full of rowers, but my mind was already far away as I thought once again of the journey that culminated to this very moment...

Chapter 1

Faithless and Frustrated

Do not deceive yourselves. If any of you think you are wise by the standards of this age, you should become "fools" so that you may become wise.

I Corinthians 3:18

"Michael, why would we go to the *Bahamas* if they already *have* the gospel? Did you hear the sermon? There are THREE BILLION people who have never heard the gospel in the world today; that's "BILLION" with a "B."

"Wow, that seems impossible."

"Yes, impossible."

Since the Holy Spirit had repeatedly murmured "Go to the Bahamas" but had never given Michael or I a plan to make that happen, we rationalized our slow response by investigating our church's campaign to send people all over the world to unreached people groups, those without the gospel. At this point we did not recognize or receive God's very clear call to go to the Bahamas and instead were looking for confirmation from others who would be more "qualified" to discern what seemed like an absurd directive.

Although I was intrigued by the concept of going to another country to share the gospel, I was not thinking I was moving to the Bahamas to become a missionary. For that matter, I had no idea what being a missionary meant or looked like. I had never been in a church that talked about missions.

Michael and I were plagued with confusion because God never articulated a clear path on how to move to the Bahamas or what to do and live. On top of this, we felt disqualified, so we sought the church's missionary 'experts.' We loved our church and were firm supporters of God's mandate to be a part of a fellowship of local believers; we knew we should seek their godly wisdom for direction and guidance. As the investigation began, we realized our home church was focused on sending people to countries where the name "Jesus" had never been heard or preached, whereas our goal was trying to determine what to do with this call. God had only told us the "where" which was the Bahamas, and this didn't make sense. They already had the gospel and were classified as "Christian" according to statistics from our church mission's department.

"Maybe we don't get it, Michael. I want to be obedient, but I have no idea how I can obey God without knowing how to survive! And becoming a missionary is not what I am signing up for! Surely, God does not want us to live in a small hut somewhere in the middle of nowhere, right?"

"Probably not. But honestly Amy, we can at least check it out."

As we considered the Mission Department's advice we were circumvented by a year of investigation as to where *else* we could go on mission. Turkey became the church's answer. However, since Jesus had repeatedly murmured, *"Go to the Bahamas,"* but had never given us a plan to make that happen, we became perplexed and paralyzed by indecision.

To confuse matters further I was not confident this call was a call to a radically different life as missionaries.

At our first meeting with the church Pastor of Missions, Kevin asked "Ok, tell me a little bit about yourselves; what do you *do* for a living?"

"Um, well we build houses and sell them."

"Oh, ok, tell me more about your family."

"Well, we have four children and we love kids," I responded.

Kevin was enthusiastic and attentive; it seemed like great affirmation to God's call to go on mission, but I was frankly terrified.

"Michael, how old is he?" I said after leaving the meeting.

"Oh maybe 25. He did say he just got married and was raised on the mission field. I think somewhere in the Caribbean where his Dad was a Pastor."

"Oh, how could he know anything about raising four kids and what our life is like? We are not in ministry and we were not raised in a Pastor's family or for that matter on the mission field. Is this crazy to be having a conversation with a virtual stranger, entrusting our lives to someone in their twenties?!"

"Come on now, Amy, let's not overreact. I thought we were just considering this, not actually doing it yet."

"This young man is theologically gifted, and I respect him, but he has no idea who we truly are as people, who our friends are, how we were raised and ultimately how there is *no way* we could be missionaries."

I took my doubts into my prayer closet. Well, actually I spent my morning prayer time debating with God, reminding Him of my amazing accomplishments. *God, you know I don't have a lot of time because of work and children but I still find time to teach Sunday school. And you know I love my Bible study, but I do have to miss work to make that happen. Lord, remember also, on my only day off, which is your day Lord, Sunday, I make a meal for the Pastors during their services and I also greet at the door of the church. Oh, and just in case you forgot Lord, I take time out of my already busy schedule to feed the homeless with my small group too. Surely, I am following You Lord, right?*

God saw my actions and heard my words, but He also saw what I did not understand, my heart justifying itself by what I did *for* Him, not by loving Him first. The Holy Spirit reminded me of Matthew 23:26 when Jesus says to the religious people, "You blind Pharisees! First clean the inside of the cup and the dish, so that the outside of it may become clean also."

In contrast, our Mission Pastor Kevin did not see anything but the outside of the cup-my façade-the persona I created. He continued to pursue this call to the mission field for my family and me, and one Sunday after church asked again if we wanted to meet to discuss things further.

At that next meeting, we also met with Kevin's associate Stewart to discuss the "further" he had mentioned.

When we finished, Michael responded, "Well we really appreciate all the time and efforts that you have spent helping us pursue this call and the recommendation of going to Turkey, but like we told you several months ago, God told us "Bahamas." In fact, He still is saying it, but we don't know what to do there and God hasn't told us either."

Kevin and Stewart looked quizzically at each other and back at us.

Michael introduced an idea we'd been considering but hadn't mentioned to them.

"We have found a place in Eleuthera where they teach Bible training and I want to take my family there to check it out."

"Oh, ok," Kevin said. "What's the name of it? I'll check it out too." But I wondered about his response by the blank look on his face. At this the conversation ended. I felt unsettled. It seemed like our missionary Pastor was unenthusiastic about helping us determine how to bring the gospel where it was already preached and taught.

"It seems like Kevin was not too keen on the idea of the Bible Training School from his response. What do you think, Hon?"

"I see what you mean. I noticed it, too," Michael answered.

"Honestly, I just feel really uncertain about it all." I was clearly frustrated.

Our confusion propelled indecision and time just kept going by with no definitive plan in place.

Since I already had a busy life and could not make sense of the myriad of details, I rationalized why it didn't make sense to just leave everything and go to the Bahamas. Mostly, embracing missionary life would be foregoing a social class that had standards of living and expectations that were just that- the "standard" necessities of life. We were used to living in a beautiful, large home in an affluent neighborhood. Having nice cars was crucial. Owning a boat and keeping it on the lake was an absolute. Sending our four children to the best schools and summer camps in Texas was also an easy *yes* in my standard equation. Adding to that frequent expensive vacations or hunting and fishing on our deer lease every weekend was a minimum requirement.

I would reason if we could not spend our time at the lease or on the boat we could at least go to Michael's parent's house on the lake or to the ranch in West Texas. Country club memberships, an abundance of after school activities, social clubs, debutante balls and board memberships were also expected. I had grown up like this and certainly I was going to raise my family the same way. Church was yet another facet of my check list. I wanted to be plugged into the right place where we could all get fed spiritually on Sunday. And we were.

One morning as we left our usual Sunday brunch at the Club, I said to Michael, "Kevin is so young; surely he cannot understand how hard we have worked to get to this place in life." It seemed we repeated this conversation between ourselves over eggs benedict every week throughout that year.

Plus, the responses we got from friends and family showed alarmed reactions filled with caution. They struggled with what this radical change in lifestyle might mean, too. "Amy this is the worst decision you would be making of your entire life," my closest relative told me one day.

A dear girlfriend pronounced one morning at Starbucks, "You will come back, I know you will, Amy," in between sips of her white chocolate mocha cappuccino. "It sounds amazing, almost dream-like to live in the Bahamas, but don't you think you will get tired of it?"

I thought of Jesus' words to His followers in Luke 14:26–27, "If anyone comes to me and does not hate his own father and mother and wife and children and brothers and sisters, yes, and even his own life, he cannot be my disciple. Whoever does not bear his own cross and come after me cannot be my disciple." This call was radical when Jesus issued it to the masses centuries ago and it is just as radical now.

When I looked at the original language of the word "hate" I discovered it means "love less." *Was I willing to forego the life I created for myself, to love it less, the life I had been taught was "normal and expected" for the unknown?* I could not understand what I was being asked to do and neither could anyone else. Consequently, Michael and I decided to do the only thing we could do: devise our own plan to satisfy God's demands. We believed God and did not want to disobey Him, but we were uncertain how to move to an entirely different and new life without a concrete plan.

Unbeknownst to us, this inward tension was God's alarm system sounding. It was the Holy Spirit beckoning us to trust and obey Him and if we would comply there would be blessing awaiting us. The Scripture in Hebrews 11:6 came to mind, "And without faith it is impossible to please him, for whoever would draw near to God must believe that he exists and that he rewards those who seek him."

Yet no one we spoke to about this mysterious commission on our lives had this discernment, so we felt somewhat crazy. We did not realize power and authority come from the Holy Spirit and that we were being chosen as instruments of service for His kingdom. Although we had been taught the importance of Jesus' command in Matthew 28:19, 20, "Therefore go and make disciples of all nations, baptizing them in the name of the Father and the Son and of the Holy Spirit, and teaching them to obey everything I have commanded you. And surely I am with you always, to the very end of the age." we had not read or been taught verse 18. Just prior to these verses Jesus states, "All authority on heaven and on earth has been given to me."

The Great Commission in the first verses is given to all followers of Jesus because of the power and authority Jesus was given by God, His Father, upon His obedience to the Father's will to die for the sins of mankind. In Luke 24:49 after Jesus' resurrection from the grave, he visits the disciples and reminds them of that same power He would now bestow on them by saying, "And behold, I am sending the promise of my Father upon you. But stay in the city until you are clothed with power from on high." And again, in John 16:7–8, Jesus explains the importance of His obedience correlating to the receiving of the Holy Spirit for those who follow Him. He says to his disciples, "Nevertheless, I am telling you the truth. It is for your benefit that I am going away, because if I don't go away, the Counselor (the Holy Spirit) will not come to you. If I go I will send him to you. When he comes he will convict the world about sin, righteousness and judgement:.." Not realizing that as believers and followers of Jesus this same power and authority had been given to us through the Holy Spirit we had no faith to step out and heed the command to "Go." We were already making disciples in our current life, serving in lots of different ways in the city of Austin, our city, so why "Go?", we concluded.

In Acts 26:17–18 Jesus clearly shows His authority and power are bestowed upon those He calls when he speaks boldly to Saul who is soon to become Paul. As Paul recounts his conversion from Saul to Paul he relays Jesus' mandate on his life when he retells what Jesus said to him as Saul. He had been sent "to open their eyes so that they may turn from darkness to light and from the power of Satan to God that they may receive forgiveness of sins and a place among those who are sanctified by the faith in me." Jesus shows that His call enables His chosen to carry out His evangelism through the power of the Holy Spirit.

Jesus also shows His authority and power is released to the seventy-two disciples He appoints and sends out. Luke chapter 10 records that as he sends them out two by two, he gives them specific details about not taking any "sandals" or "purse," which in our modern-day times would be money or clothing. He then goes on to say in verse 9, "Heal the sick who are there and tell them, 'The kingdom of God has come near to you.'"

The result of their obedience is clear as told in verse 17, "The seventy-two returned with joy and said, "Lord, even the demons submit to us in your name." The power of abiding and obeying are clear when Jesus articulates a mandate on your life.

We realized our delay at responding to God's call at this time in our lives was actually disobedience. Our problem was we had no understanding that our unknowing and disqualifications were the exact recipe for success God wanted. The eventual result would be that His authority given and used in our family would reveal His power and glory, not our own glory.

As 2006 crept into 2007 and finally 2008, we lived by our own worldly rationale and executed a strategy that we thought would eventually get us into a financial situation where we could move to the Bahamas. *Let us make a lot of money Lord, let us save up so we can have provision, and then we will come and follow You*, we'd pray. This seemed reasonable in our estimation. We could plan to move and have enough money to live for a while so that we could see what the Lord really wanted us to do. With this plan now concretely in place, we continued our day to day–work, kids, school, church.

But mostly work. The way to execute this plan would be to capitalize on a booming real estate market. Since Michael and I both had careers in this field we knew we could labor hard for several years, saving up enough money for ourselves so that we could obey the Lord's call. Or so we thought....

What we did not yet understand is that when God Almighty places a call on your life, He will make it happen. Michael and I didn't realize our lack of faith was the catalyst for our lives to unravel. Yet God in His mercy knew what it would take to make me willing. He alone would take my mustard seed of faith by taking me on a journey of purification. He would allow me to determine who I was and if I was going to align myself with who my identity portrayed or who my mind wanted to believe I was as Amy Boykin.

My refinement was to begin by removing idols that usurped God's position as number one in my heart. Undetected strongholds abounded, and God was about to demolish them whether I liked it or not. He began orchestrating circumstances that would force me to make choices. As He peeled away the layers of my life, the very things I *thought* had no bearing on who I was, I found my very identity was also being stripped away from me. I hadn't realized these ideas, objects, and relationships had a grip on me. But God saw my unbelieving heart and hard-headedness and unleashed the refinement process. The only question was would I be able to endure it?

Chapter 2

Fame and Fortune or Empty Cisterns?

For my people have done two evil things:
They have abandoned me-the fountain of living water.
And they have dug for themselves cracked cisterns that
can hold no water at all!

Jeremiah 2:13

"Amy, where should I start? This empty dining room is pointless. I need a bigger laundry room too. Most importantly, since I work from home, I need a small office that allows me privacy while I also can watch the kids play in the playroom. Any ideas?"

My friend Charlotte was one of my first design clients. I wrote down a laundry list of her needs, took measurements of the rooms, and devised a master plan of how to accomplish the goals given her budget.

My love of space planning and a high priority in maintaining good relationships had caused my business to grow from designing spaces to remodeling homes. This new dimension led me to find great subcontractors to do the construction as I oversaw the project as the general contractor. Attention to detail and an outgoing personality were a recipe for rapid success in the male-dominated industry of construction. What had begun strictly as a design firm grew into a design/build company. Christian characteristics of integrity and honesty were the trademarks of my success.

However, God was nudging me to put on the brakes, but I didn't see it at first.

"4:30 am. Really Amy?" Michael leaned over, pulling the sheets over his head.

"Oh honey," I whispered, "I have to be home for the kids to make them breakfast then take them to preschool. You know that."

By then he would be back to sleep snoring. After dressing in the dark, I tip-toed out the door to my suburban and would drive to the office feeling satisfied. *Yes, I could do it all*, I would think. Day after day this was my routine. By 7 am I would be back home, so I could wake my children and do what all good Mommies do: prepare their meals, bathe them, dress them, pack their lunch and take them to school.

At this time in my life, I had been studying what it looks like to live as a Christian woman according to Proverbs Chapter 31. Verses 15–17 say, "She gets up while it is still night; she provides food for her family and portions for her female servants. She considers a field and buys it; out of her earnings she plants a vineyard. She sets about her work vigorously;

her arms are strong for her tasks." Like the verses illustrate, this woman can do it all and I was on a mission to be just like her, getting up early and using my strong arms to serve my family. Yes, I worked hard to provide for my family spiritually, physically and emotionally.

Unfortunately, my career was my number one priority, not God and His plan. I did not realize the word "fear" in Proverbs 31 meant to put the Lord first; first in your heart so everything else overflowed from Him. It was clear the only thing I feared was not attending to my successful business.

As my clients and projects grew in my design/build firm, I was reaping the benefits of the American dream and expanded further, building new homes instead of simply remodeling existing homes. Eventually Michael came on as my chief financial officer and together we led this booming business. Soon I was able to forego clients altogether and build speculative homes that I could design and sell.

As I worked on the first project, it went under contract before I even broke ground on construction. Inwardly I jumped for joy at this newfound success, *Amy you did it!* I congratulated myself. But God knew my heart and saw how I idolized myself. Fearing Him was not part of the picture. I took ownership of my strengths and victories; the very talents God had blessed me with. The concept God had given me, to design and build new homes to look and feel like old homes, was unheard of in Austin at this time. This business practice led to worldly achievement and I became an overnight success.

It was all part of God's plan but the ascent to success became my persona-who I was. Although I thought I was living like that Proverbs 31 woman, it was the *why* behind the doing that betrayed my soul. I was not doing these things to honor Christ but honor myself. The awards and high-end sale prices gave me an inward entitlement that became my identity.

Accolades like being a designer of a HGTV Dream home and being featured multiple times in InStyle Home and Austin Monthly were not helpful. These very public accomplishments would have been the perfect occasion to give all the glory to the Lord, but, my heart betrayed my words and I ended up promoting myself. I had become prideful, although at the time, I had no idea this was the true state of my heart.

Juggling these emotions wrecked me as I justified my behavior to the Lord. *I must work like this so we can afford to live in the Bahamas when we move.* Yes, the call to the Bahamas was still being whispered in my prayer time. Both Michael and I still knew this was God's design for us, but we were chasing after it in our own strength.

There was also more confusion as I prayed every day for the Lord to allow me to stay at home exclusively with my children. I knew I was going to look up and my children would be eighteen and off to college and I would have missed the most precious years of their lives. Outwardly I loved the notoriety of my newfound fame but inwardly the chaos and confusion from trying to do it all left me exhausted.

No wonder I was exhausted, my life had become full of idols and emptiness like the Jeremiah scripture spoke of in 2:13 saying, "For my people have done two evil things: They have abandoned me-the fountain of living water. And they have dug for themselves cracked cisterns that can hold no water at all!" It wasn't just that I had formed my own ideas and plans about how to achieve a life of fulfillment but also that I had fallen prey to putting my heart on them as my treasure. I was disillusioned because I did not quench my thirst with Christ who alone could fill me up. I was misled by the deceitfulness of a worldly system that was a lie and never would give me inward contentment or joy I was longing for.

My strategy to achieve financial gain so we could go on mission for the Lord had revealed my fallen, sinful self. As the Lord had allowed my three-year-old company to build over twenty-five million-dollar homes, I became conceited. Then came the real estate market downturn in 2008 and we were left with four unsold houses, "empty cisterns," all listed for well over one million dollars. Finally, I began to crash as the market crashed. I was forlorn and exhausted, crushed by the weight of all the pressure to succeed.

As these houses sat empty waiting for a buyer, I saw they were a lifeless void and my barren soul looked just like these vacant houses. The fact they weren't selling made me realize I had to face decisions and quickly. *How would we afford to live without the sale of these homes, God?* We could not afford even our own house payments. Thankfully

God intervened in His God-like way when a famous TV personality unexpectedly approached Michael and I and made us an offer on our newly built personal home but now I was deflated. The financial relief was much needed and allowed us to live but Michael and I had thought in due time we would sell our house and use this profit for our eventual move to the Bahamas not for daily survival. *Why Lord?* I cried. *Why have I been killing myself to store up enough money to obey your call when this is not happening as I planned?*

One by one, I knew I had to let go of things. The boat, the deer lease, the vacations, club memberships, the expensive schools, dance lessons and camps, everything. I quickly saw myself going with them. *Who am I, Lord!? These things never really meant anything to me, you know that, but I feel like I'm disappearing.* Finally, God took me to a place I would have to face on my own.

If I thought all this had been difficult, I was about to face the real me. This situation would force me to declare obedience or disobedience to God's call.

The only thing that kept me going was my husband Michael and our marriage. But even that relationship was crumbling, and I now cried out to the Lord. *What will I do, Lord; oh, what will I do?*

Chapter 3

Idols and Altars

Therefore, my beloved, flee idolatry.

1 Corinthians 10:14

Although our marriage foundation had begun in Jesus it was not centered on Him at all. When I first fell in love in 1985, I was a freshman in high school. I had given Michael my heart, and all of it. As we sat under the full moon next to the pool at the club, I asked, "Michael Boykin, do you believe in Jesus?"

"What?" he laughed. "What in the world do you mean, Amy?"

"Well, I mean, do you really know Jesus as your Lord and Savior? I know you go to church, but do you truly believe in Him, in Jesus?"

"Um, well yeah, I guess."

"You don't sound so confident, Michael. I just need you to know I will not date anyone who does not believe in Jesus."

"Really?"

"Yes, really." I moved off his chest and looked directly into his eyes.

I knew the Lord and had a personal relationship with Him. I had committed myself to Jesus the year before and I was learning and growing in the word of God. I was convinced that my faith was going to be the foundation of my life. I also wanted to date someone who felt the same way. If this boy, Michael Boykin, that I was cuddling with at the country club wanted me to date him, he better believe in Jesus.

Michael hesitated then said, "Okay, tell me more. Maybe I don't really *"know"* Jesus like you are asking me."

"Michael, we all need, Jesus. We are sinful and even born in sin. Jesus came as the Son of God and died for not only my sins but all of mankind's. He stood in my place and was the sacrifice for me.

"Why?" Michael asked.

I proceeded to tell Michael God's plan of salvation from the Scripture and asked him if he wanted to surrender his life to Christ. I was so grateful he responded with a 'yes,' and we bowed our heads in prayer.

Now here we were twenty-four years later. We had the Holy Spirit and knew His voice, yet we were actually being disobedient. We had no idea that accepting Jesus was something totally different than following Him daily, and the only way to obey Him was to *do* what He said when He said it. In 2 Corinthians 5:7, Paul says "For we walk by faith and not by sight." We did not realize this is what Jesus was asking of us at the time.

As my refinement process of removing the idols in my life was nearing completion, I was now thinking back to that first unofficial "date" we had in high school and wondered if I could stay in the covenant commitment, I had made in my marriage so many years ago.

As our sin of trusting in ourselves instead of God became apparent, I began to see I had sought Michael for comfort and refuge instead of God. At the same time, I would vehemently fault Michael for this disastrous state our family was now living in. Letting go of the world's idea of success humbled me and at the same time made me mad that my husband could not provide for us as the world ascribes. Blame was the name of my game and I did not realize I too had a big role in this calamity. I had abandoned my family and was not present in any way, shape or form. I had worked tirelessly over the years to make money for "the call" God had articulated, but I had lost sight of what God had placed right before my eyes—my precious family.

As the Real Estate market crashed in 2008, my marriage collapsed and emotionally I was ambivalent. Instead of turning to Michael to help and console him, I turned against him. 'For better or worse' from my wedding vows was becoming hard to endure as the 'worse' was endless arguments. Round and round we went. Even though we repented and forgave each other, the fighting left me empty and distance grew between us. Scars left me wounded and betrayed and I hardly knew if I could go on with the life I created, my marriage or Michael.

Seeking godly counsel at our home church, we plugged away at our marriage, not realizing that God was trying to get our attention. We still knew the call He had placed on our lives but now it looked impossible although we still heard *"Go"* repetitively in our prayer time. Even more confirmation was occurring. Although Michael and I had repeatedly questioned God's voice and command to move to the Bahamas, we gained more confidence in His will for us when God confirmed it in the word-the Bible.

We had been studying and applying a sermon series on the book of Genesis from our home church in Austin. We wholeheartedly believe in the inerrancy of Scripture and knew God was speaking to us directly.

He confirmed that Abraham's calling was to be our calling while I was listening to my Pastor preach from Genesis 11.

One Sunday morning, as I heard verse 31 read out loud, "...and they went forth together from Ur of the Chaldees to go into the land of Canaan..." I froze in my seat. *This is it,* I said to myself. The Holy Spirit was illuminating the Word in my heart. *This is to apply to me and our call,* I said as I there motionless. At this moment I comprehended God was telling me that Austin was akin to the sophisticated idol-worshipping city of "Ur of the Chaldees" and that we were to leave it for somewhere in the Bahamas. The murmurs of going that had begun in 2006 were now clearly articulated in the word of God.

God's telling us to "Go" both in prayer and the Word, to move away from what we thought our life was to be, would provide the faith to trust Him for His plan for our life. Although our extended family and the life we had created were in Austin, God, who is never arbitrary, was so very kind to remind me of other scripture He had spoken about our call. As I reviewed my prayer journal from our Bahamas vacation in August of 2006, I saw God had given me another scripture about Abraham when He initially whispered *Move to the Bahamas.*

Looking back over my notes, there was Hebrews 11:8, "By faith Abraham, when he was called, obeyed by going out to a place which he was to receive an inheritance, and he went out, not knowing where he was going." It was like a light bulb turned on in my head! As I saw these words and put the pieces of this puzzle all together, I realized these two scriptures combined with the Holy Spirit's whispers of "Go" clearly meant God wanted us to take a leap of faith and trust Him alone! Finally, I had to submit to God!

Of course, the enemy must have seen my final resolve and kept sneaking up behind me with lies and doubt. *Amy, you're a mess and your marriage is still a mess. Your real problem is not you but Michael.* I started believing the lies and thinking by the world, *I need to just start over. My marriage is a disaster. And if I do, I can have that awesome life back and all the success I worked for.*

Satan was doing everything possible to deceive me. One crucial trick was reminding me of the acclaim and stature I had and how I could easily maintain it by staying put in Austin. He made me think that the life I had been purified from was really my true happiness and contentment. *That is really who you are, Amy,* I would hear him sneer. *This is your very identity, why would you ever consider leaving this life?* He would taunt me. The lies continued, with thoughts that Michael was beyond repair, I was beyond repair, our marriage was in a state of calamity and finally that our idol worshipping hearts made us unworthy of any "missionary status."

Deflated, I finally understood that my foundation had been placed in Michael and my marriage and this was the ultimate idol of my life. As I came to terms with this new revelation, I quickly realized that the root of all my wrong thinking was placing hope and confidence in anything and everything but Jesus. Exposing my treasure seeking heart shook me to my core. After months of crying over the pain of forgoing things in order to stay financially and emotionally secure, the thought of losing my husband awakened me to the desperate state I was now in. Now the only thing that mattered was repenting and believing God could and would change my heart and forgive me for making my husband my God, instead of my suitor helper.

My marriage was hanging on by a thread—I had nothing to lose.

This was it. Would I believe Satan feeding me lies about myself or would I believe God and who He told me I was to become in Christ? I had to decide first and foremost if I would give up on my covenant commitment of marriage. I realized I worshiped Michael and our marriage by placing hope and confidence in it and in him instead of in Jesus. The gospel of grace was unknown to me and I did not understand that grace by faith was the justification of who I am in Christ. The fact that my life was to be a continuous process of repentance and forgiveness not only for myself but for Michael would have been a true testament to Jesus, but I did not understand *yet.*

Another crucial misstep in my faith was not recognizing who believers are when we profess faith in Jesus. 2 Corinthians 5:17 clearly states, "Therefore, if anyone is in Christ, he is a new creation. The old has passed away; behold, the new has come." The new me was "in Christ" and that meant everything Christ has I now have. Trying to fix or clean up the old me who had died with Jesus on the cross for me did nothing to secure my newness in Him today.

As I learnt biblical teaching on Romans 6, the Holy Spirit opened my heart to this understanding: the old me died with Jesus when He bore all my sin on the cross. Verse 11 says, "So you also must consider yourselves dead to sin and alive to God in Christ Jesus." Being alive meant I could not concentrate on the dead-old me or Michael. I had to ascribe the new characteristic of Jesus to myself and Michael in order to understand how Christ already sees us. This realization led to other revelations, too.

Since Michael was my treasure, as was my marriage, I had mistakenly focused on how to change myself and Michael by fixating on our problems instead of ascribing and meditating on God's attribute within each of us as new creations in Jesus. Looking at how God sees us in Christ birthed life and hope but sadly at this time in my life I would come to my knees night after night for over a year, crying. I begged God to heal my marriage and family, telling Him I in return would do whatever it took to obey Him. I had made an internal ultimatum: *Would I give up on my marriage, my husband's and our life together, and our family? Had my disobedience to God's command been the precipice for the consistent removal of a life I had worked so hard for year after year?* These questions swirled in my head but still, there was more to come. In the middle of this upheaval, I realized that indeed my identity had been in answers to those very things in lieu of trusting Jesus.

After much prayer and continual pleading with God, I searched scripture for answers.

I looked intently at my marriage vows; the commitment I had made to God first and foremost. I saw in the Bible that God initiates the covenant of marriage "and the two shall become one flesh," as Scripture says in Ephesians 5:31. It wasn't Amy Boykin who brought Michael and I together, it was God. *Could I trust God now to keep us together?* I cried repeatedly. Verse 32 goes on to say, "This mystery is profound, and that I am saying it refers to Christ and the church." *What did God mean by this?* I would wonder.

When the Holy Spirit finally brought me to the realization that I valued my marriage and Michael more than Him and His call I had an epiphany. I knew I could never fix Michael, or his sin nor could he fix me or my sin. Whatever idol we allowed to take the place of Jesus in our heart would be a sin. I began to see that God uses sin to be sand paper to one another as our individual sanctification process and with us as a couple. As Christ forgave me repeatedly, I too was to forgive Michael and vice versa.

The "mystery" was the grace that Christ accomplished by dying for me and granting me a life of sanctification and glorification. I too must live with the same grace towards Michael and address the new man we both were "in Christ" in every situation, versus trying to address the dead, sinful man. This revelation prompted me to decide I would trust Him to this life and to the call he had given in 2006. I did not know if Michael would change or I would change. I did not know if our sins would keep a hold on us or if this call was the answer to freedom, but I did know I was going to trust God and live by Him. I would honor my wedding vows and honor the call. I knew I loved the Lord the most and I knew now who I was "in Christ."

God knew it would take purification to get my attention. He had taken me on this four-year journey, so I would show Him I believed Him, that I would trust Him, that I would keep my commitment to my marriage despite our sins and failures, allowing Jesus to use it all for His glory.

One night I prayed earnestly, *God I will give you everything now. I will trust you with it all.* I whispered. Satan also whispered back, *Will you really Amy?*

Chapter 4

The Narrow Path

The apostles said to the Lord, "Increase our faith!" And the Lord said, "If you had faith like a grain of mustard seed, you could say to this mulberry tree, 'Be uprooted and planted in the sea,' and it would obey you.'

Luke 17:5–6

Throughout our four years of indecision, Michael and I had been asking God just exactly which Bahamian island He had in mind. Although for many years we had visited the island of Exuma, we were concerned about not being able to have neighbors with whom to fellowship, since it is sparsely populated with few towns separated by long distances.

"Where did these people find friends?" we asked each other. "How did the locals have community?"

The years we had spent vacationing on Exuma had given us great memories of rest and laughter as a family but as we began to look at living somewhere full time we thought about larger issues. A neighborhood to live in, a school for our kids and a church to worship at became paramount.

When we returned home from Exuma we realized it did not meet the criteria we desired so we began to pray, "Where Lord?"

We knew the lack of peace was an indication of pursuing a different plan and looking for God's will, so we continued to ask, *What is most important, Lord? Are we on the right track in our thinking?* The Holy Spirit told us being a part of a church community would be of utmost importance since we had no idea what we were going to do for a living.

As we searched scripture for what church community looked like in the New Testament, we were reminded of the Apostle Paul's encouragement to the Philippian believers, "Then make me truly happy by agreeing whole-heartedly with each other, loving one another, and working together with one mind and purpose" (Philippians 2:2). We knew these words were to guide us so we asked God to place us on an island in the Bahamas where people believed in Him and where we could be burden bearers and encouragers to others living out the Christian life. We were hoping and praying to be able to work, but we were uncertain what that looked like or even if it meant working in ministry on some level. We were still not yet to the point of calling ourselves "missionaries."

Step one would be to find the right island. Step two would be God showing His will for us wherever we lived. Every decision required complete abandon to Him and God wanted us to trust Him step by step by faith.

In July of 2008, just before the Real Estate market crash in November, we decided to visit the Bahamian island of Eleuthera. One of the biggest reasons for the visit was to check out the Eleuthera Bible Training Institute we had mentioned to our church mission Pastor. We had found it online but had no idea what they did and if this was indeed where God wanted to plant our family.

* * * * * * *

Once we landed and got settled, we immediately called the Institute and set up a meeting. A couple of days later, we traveled about an hour up the winding road of Eleuthera to the Institute. After welcoming us in, we learned during our conversation that the Institute trained and equipped local pastors and clergy with courses that yielded seminary credit. We were deflated; we knew this was not our expertise. We were not theologians and not ready to teach and equip such prestigious men and women. But as we sat with the precious missionary couple, Stephen and Mary Ann Glover, they asked us what we were looking for in a city.

"Have you considered Spanish Wells?" they asked. "We just finished a Bible course there and we have great friends at the local church there as well."

Upon their recommendation, we decided on our next vacation we would take their advice and travel to Spanish Wells.

In May of 2009 we returned to Eleuthera. Spanish Wells is a smaller island off Eleuthera only three and a half miles long with approximately fifteen hundred inhabitants. From the minute we stepped foot on the island we felt peace and joy everywhere we went. We immediately knew these feelings, coupled with the presence of a community, were an answer to our prayers! We were grateful God also confirmed our decision when we attended the church the Glovers had recommended. It was at that Sunday service where we heard a sermon on "Christ Alone" that we knew we were indeed home! We finally committed to beginning our new life in this small community. Yet doing this would require me to trust God with complete abandon. This unfamiliar way of doing life was the beginning of living in the unseen. I knew faith was the substance of things hoped for and the conviction of things not seen from Hebrews 11:1 but what I was about to learn was that faith required obedience.

After we returned home from the trip, I looked at scripture about faith and saw repeatedly that God called unknown, normal people to big tasks.

Looking at the story of Noah who built the ark required action. Looking at Mary, I thought about how difficult it must have been to carry a baby when she was a virgin and not married.

Living faith was active and required making choices that showed full confidence that God would do the very thing He said He would do. Time and time again as I looked through the Hebrew's list of the heroes of faith in Chapter 11, I saw this common thread of regular, everyday people doing something that must have seemed crazy at the time when God spoke to them to do it.

Okay Lord, I can and will do this. My resolve was final, and relief now washed over me. I knew without a doubt that we would be moving to Spanish Wells.

A few days later we returned to Austin from the Eleuthera trip and I had a new inward conviction which gave me confidence to move full steam ahead. I was ready to tackle my "to do" moving list with zeal. We had only two months of summer to close down our company, terminate our current house lease, and unenroll the kids from school. At the same time, we would be figuring out all the logistics of life in the Bahamas. From the get-go, our resolve was being tested; we were immediately thrown for a loop.

"What do you mean, Michael!?"

We had returned home from our trip confident the house we had found and rented for the upcoming year would at least provide us security to move to the Bahamas. We also knew we could not back out. Now here was Michael calling to tell me the nice Bahamian couple had changed their mind and would no longer rent us the house.

"But we just shipped three pallets of toys and books to the island, Michael!" I had tears rolling down my face. I was driving while talking on my cell phone and couldn't do both. I pulled over to collect myself and finish the conversation.

"Look, Amy, it will be fine. You know God told me to rent that vacation home on the beach, so we could acclimate to this big move and unpack and get settled. This must have been why."

"What do you mean, Michael?" I choked back my tears.

"Well, obviously our best laid plans are not God's. He will give us another house on the island once we arrive in a few weeks."

"You really think we will find one? There were only a few furnished houses that would even consider renting long term, Michael."

"Absolutely. Let me pray for us now and it will be fine. Trust, Amy, trust."

As Michael closed in prayer, I stared at the beautiful tree lined street we lived on and thought, *these houses all have kids my children have grown up with and attended school with, Lord. They are used to the security of this life.* As my mind wandered, I already was questioning this decision. I pleaded with God. *This is too much. I cannot move myself and my four young children to a country without work, without a permanent residence, and without a plan, God. Please!*

Somehow, someway I went onward. God was teaching me that living by faith meant decisions and behaviors had to align continuously. It was obvious now during the final stages of moving, that God placed us exactly where He wanted us-totally dependent on Him to provide everything we needed physically, spiritually and financially. I was beginning to understand this new journey was like Paul says in Romans 1:17, "For in it (the gospel) the righteousness of God is revealed from faith for faith, as it is written, "The righteous shall live by faith." *Would my life really be "right" with Christ if I could trust Him? Live by Him?* "Amy, you can do this, yes you can," I repeated to myself out loud over and over again.

As I embraced this way of surrendered living, the summer flew by until finally we were down to weeks until we would officially bid the USA bon voyage. Our departure would be finalized with a huge Moving and Estate sale. Although now we did not have a house to move into in the Bahamas, we did have enough sense to know that whatever house we found, along with the new life that was forthcoming, would require money and lots of it since we had no employment. We decided the best way to make money would be to sell everything we had amassed over our lifetime.

Although we had hoped the four speculative homes we had built would sell by now, they had not. Gratefully we were able to rent them for a year and felt confident they would eventually sell. Then, we reasoned, we would have more money to live on. But for now, everything had to go.

Friends and family had helped market and organize the sale and for weeks we had been preparing and praying. Even our children's valued possessions were being sold. We wanted them all to be excited about the move and get used to the change of lifestyle from America to the Bahamas. It began with our oldest son Luke; his plethora of toys from a Wii to an iPod would be unnecessary for our new life and for that matter any eight-year-old.

At first, Luke had whined about selling his treasures, but I used it all for God's new plan.

"Luke, we won't need any of these "things" in the Bahamas. God wants us to embark upon a new plan where we can be with Him more" I would say. "Remember all of those fishing trips we have been on? We hope to go on more, so you won't need your games or electronics anymore!"

"Oh, Mama are you sure?" Luke replied. I hoped my convincing had worked.

Finally, the long-awaited day came for the Estate Sale. It surprisingly began much earlier than I expected. I gently shook my eldest son Luke awake. He didn't stir so I finally whispered in his ear, "Luke!"

"What, Mama?" his soft voice mumbled.

"Someone is looking at your toys, honey."

"But it's dark outside."

"Yes, I know sweetheart, but we already have people here who want to look at your Wii, and remember you said you wanted to sell it yourself."

"What?!" He leapt up, threw off the covers and turned on the lights.

Three-year-old James and five-year-old Josie also shared the room.

"Turn off the lights!" they hollered.

But Luke, who shared Michael's business savvy, wanted to make the most of the sales opportunity. He walked out of the room in his Spider-man undies. "Where'd you put the Wii Mama? Where are the people?"

"Um son, first put on some shorts and a shirt. The people are in the living room."

Since the day started off well with a big Wii sale, the rest of the kids jumped out of bed joyfully to see what all *they* could sell for their new Bahamian adventure. Michael and I devised a plan and issued a grand prize for the winner who could sell the most of their own things.

"Mommy, what will we win?" Marley, my seven-year-old daughter, asked.

"I don't know you will just have to see. Something great though! Maybe a trip to... guess where Marley?"

"Where Mama?" said my mature oldest daughter.

"The Bahamas!" I laughed.

"Oh Mommy, isn't that where we are moving anyway?"

She also questioned me repeatedly, "Why can't we take the trampoline, Mommy?!"

Sweet Josie, my five-year-old, was the only one quite content to sell it all as long as we made it to the Bahamas with her special pillow she snuggled with nightly. But our three-year-old toddler James was heartbroken not to be able to take his new pet turtle, Hank.

Days before the Estate Sale we had a farewell party for Hank as we took him down to the creek and said a prayer for him and his new life. Putting on a good show, I turned my head away while tears welled up in my eyes. As we said a family prayer for Hank and released him into the creek I constantly doubted if I could really give this life away.

The morning of the Estate Sale I had wondered; *Can I sell this doll my Grandmother left me?* I wanted to pass it to my girls or future grandchildren, God. But as the day went on, I knew it all had to go. *Amy how silly you are, you don't even have grandchildren yet.* I said to myself. Throughout the day, I would repeat Matthew 6:21, *"...for where your treasure is, there your heart will be also"* as a pep talk to bolster my confidence.

Quickly noon approached, and the sale was in full swing with my children joyfully telling neighbors, friends, and strangers that we were moving to the Bahamas. "Wow, that must be so nice," I overheard one stranger reply to the girls. "And what will your Mommy and Daddy do there?" she asked.

"Oh, I don't know and neither do they!" Josie said.

"Oh, really? That is very interesting. They must have you well provided for then."

"Oh, I don't know," Marley said with a puzzled look. "But I do know we have to sell all of our toys, so we can "survive" as my Mommy says in the Bahamas."

The stranger looked curiously at the girls and then somewhat smiling said, "Oh, well, I guess that is good."

I turned away after overhearing the conversation. *Oh Lord, can I really do this?!* Other friends came throughout the day and more offhand comments were forthcoming although most who attended were excited and encouraging.

However, some comments by neighbors were like a stake through my heart when I overheard two girlfriends.

"How can Amy give up everything? Especially with four young children?"

"I know. And neither she nor Michael have a job."

Those in our close friend group who thought they knew us best would try to assure my already unsteady mind by saying, "Amy, don't worry, it's not like you don't have a great business. If you wanted to, you could pick up right where you left off."

Their tone tried to instill confidence but only made me a nervous wreck. No one could believe we would turn away from the American dream we had built and were living. Even after all the idols had been removed, our life still looked like a great accomplishment to most.

Thankfully God supplied me with two close friends who encouraged me by saying things like, "Amy this is going to work out." And, "It may seem crazy, but I know God will provide for you."

My best friend Diana said, "You know this is really going to be great!" And because of the way she said it I believed her. God knew exactly who to use to give me assurance and throughout the day I would reflect on Diana's comments when others spoke in quieted tones as they saw me approaching. *What did they know anyway?* I would say to myself.

* * * * * * *

Days became a blur those last weeks until we made it to "V-Day." I had named it that because I knew it was my Victory. Yet climbing in my mother's big Escalade at 3 am that Saturday morning in August with our 12 bags in tow surely did not make me feel triumphant.

"Mama," Luke said. "Why are we leaving so early?"

"Well, we have four planes and a long day ahead of us, so we must arrive early at the airport to get on our first plane, Luke."

"Four planes," little Josie said, holding up five fingers.

Smiling back at her I gently strapped her in the car seat as Michael heaved our bags into the car. My Mom was already weeping at the steering wheel as we got everyone situated. Pulling away from the house I had grown up in for most of my childhood, I could hardly believe I was embarking upon this journey. *This is it, we're actually going,* I silently thought. After four years of indecision my faith was real. No more was I living by words alone. My heartfelt resolve was being put into action. I was finally beginning to understand I could only truly trust God if I was willing to do the very thing, He had beckoned me to so long ago.

As I leaned my head back and closed my eyes to pray, the Holy Spirit comforted me and gave me courage and peace that would be needed in the upcoming days.

Chapter 5

We've Arrived!
(Or So We Thought)

And blessed is she who believed that there would be a fulfillment of what was spoken to her from the Lord.

Luke 1:45

We made it to Spanish Wells late Saturday afternoon after navigating the Austin airport, Houston airport, Miami airport, Nassau airport and finally the Eleuthera airport. Michael, the children and I were exhausted, hot and very sweaty.

As we landed on the runway in our small eighteen-seater plane, we saw one small building and pulled directly up to it. Soon we would walk off this plane to a new way of life.

"This is it?" said Luke.

"What do you mean honey?" I responded.

"It's just a small house," said Luke.

"No, no, it is the airport building and we have to go through that "house" to get our passports stamped and catch a taxi to the dock."

"What do you mean, dock?" Luke asked.

"Well after about a thirty-minute taxi ride, we will take a small boat to Spanish Wells. We catch the boat at the dock."

"How long will a boat take, Mommy? I am tired and hungry. When can we eat?" said Marley.

"My thoughts exactly," Michael chimed in. Let's get this show on the road. Hurry up and exit the plane, doodlebug."

"Come on crew," I spoke back. "The boat from here to Spanish Wells should not take more than ten minutes."

"Why did we have to move somewhere that takes so long to get to, Mama?" complained Luke.

"Well, this is where God is planting us, and we have to grow as a family wherever He says."

About an hour later and exactly eighteen hours after we left my Mom's house in Austin, we finally lugged our twelve suitcases from the boat (also known as a water taxi) onto the dock of Spanish Wells.

The beach vacation house Michael had wisely rented for one week back in May when we vacationed here was a welcome relief after the taxing travel day we had experienced. Now, because of Michael's foresight, we could vacation and use this time to search for a new rental house since ours had fallen through. Our best-laid plans of our first Bahamian rental house had vanished and we were about to find the home God had chosen for us.

Of course, this was the very position God wanted me in so that He could prove His faithfulness. Removing the "me" and allowing the "He" to lead was being realized in my heart.

The beginning of the rental search process did not go well. Everywhere we went, all we heard was "No, no, no!" from locals.

"What is this family doing here?" they whispered and "Who are they, really?"

The residents of Spanish Wells were not accustomed to foreigners coming for extended stays. In fact, we were the first people who just up and moved to this tiny island without a justifiable reason or at least some church affiliated work bringing us. This lobster fishing community was filled with generational families where everyone knew each other and their entire life history.

In the Bahamas you cannot work legally without sponsorship from a Bahamian business or Bahamian organization. No wonder they were suspicious. Questions surrounded us about how we could live and not have jobs to provide income. Interestingly, I too was asking those same questions. *God, do you really want us here? If so, please provide us with a house, I begged.*

As the week continued, word got out that some Americans with four small children needed a house. The problem was the "four small children." Children meant messes and accidents. Spanish Wells was a pristine community that likes order and cleanliness. I was continually anxious, and my prayers showed it. *Is this it, God? Surely, you will not leave us nor forsake us?* I cried to Him waiting for answers and results. Tangible answers are what my entire life had been founded upon; I liked knowing what to expect. This was my mantra of success. However, God was pressing me into the unknown. Although I had enough confidence to move to the Bahamas based on the direct scriptures God had given from the Bible, He was now stretching my faith beyond what I could ever imagine.

The week of our search quickly went by and Michael and I only had one option left. It was a vacation home that a native Bahamian family owned and used when they traveled from Nassau to Spanish Wells. Michael and I prayed and prayed.

"This is it-our last and only option. But the listing price is three times over the amount we can pay, Michael," I said nervously.

"Well let's pray again before you call and just see what the Lord says," Michael responded.

I slowly dialed the number on the listing, a Mrs. Carmichael.

"Mrs. Carmichael? Yes, this is Amy Boykin. Yes, we are interested in renting your house long-term, but we have one issue," I said, almost holding my breath.

She asked me what the question was and then the flood gates opened. I began pouring out our entire journey up until that very moment, "...so you see Mrs. Carmichael, I pray you will consider lowering the price because we really want and need the house."

I was certain she was stunned by my honesty and total reliance on the Lord for this journey, but she seemed quite undisturbed by it all. I was surprised by her response, "Oh yes, yes, I do understand Mrs. Boykin, I also have four children and my husband and I are Christians. I have not experienced your situation but let me see what my husband thinks and call you back."

"Oh, and how much did you say you could afford, again?" Mrs. Carmichael asked.

I had not told her yet and closed my eyes tightly while mentioning a number that was one third of her listing price.

"Oh, ok," she said immediately. "I will call later tonight."

"Wonderful, Mrs. Carmichael and thank you so much," I replied with relief in my voice.

"Michael, she said 'tonight.' What will we do?" I sighed.

"What do you mean, Amy? We will wait until she calls back."

"But tomorrow at 8 am we have to check out of this beach house?!" I was frantic.

"Well, I guess that means God will give us the house then Amy," Michael responded.

Clearly, our journey of faith was still unfolding. *Did I have the mustard seed God asked for to move this mountain*, I wondered. I couldn't understand Michael's easy-going manner. *How come my husband seems unaffected by this situation but I cannot seem to let go and trust the Lord?*

My very identity was wrapped up in what I was sure of, a known life and a known plan. But now it seemed like all God was telling me to do was to trust Him for today alone. I recalled Scripture from Matthew 6: 34, "Therefore do not be anxious about tomorrow, for tomorrow will be anxious for itself. Sufficient for the day is its own trouble."

Okay, Lord but how do I do that? I wondered. I opened my Bible and saw right before this verse was one of my favorites from Matthew 6:33. "But seek first the kingdom of God and his righteousness, and all these things will be added unto you." *That's ironic. I saw a car that drove by with the same scripture on the side of it today*, I thought. Obviously, God is telling me this is important. Suddenly, these words lit up as the Holy Spirit illuminated what God was trying to teach me. I was beginning to understand that living in His kingdom meant taking full advantage of the blessing of *today*. Being distracted about tomorrow takes away from the opportunity of God's *right now*.

I knew that James 4:14 says, *"For what is your life? It is even a vapor that appears a little time and vanishes away."* Slowly I put these pieces together through the Holy Spirit's guidance and understood I needed to be grateful for the blessing of *today* with my family. Today, I needed to live for Jesus. To embrace with thanks the grace God was affording me through Jesus for this new life He gifted me.

There wasn't much we could do while we waited for Mrs. Carmichael's call so I quickly, grabbed the kids and Michael and told them we needed to take our beach chairs out near the water. I wanted to could enjoy God's beautiful sunset and relish in His creation. No complaints were issued by my team and as we plopped down the children began racing on the beach, singing, and dancing. Michael and I held hands and prayed, thanking the Lord for His righteousness and faithfulness to us.

A new chapter had begun. God was giving my family and me a new life and making a strong statement about what it would be like for us all.

The next morning, I ran to the grocery store to buy some baked goods and as I was standing in the check-out line waiting for the cashier, I picked up a book placed next to the gum and candy section. The title was *Eleuthera, the Island of Freedom*. Thumbing through the pages I saw that the first settlers of the island came from Europe to gain religious freedom and that they had given the land the name "Eleuthera" which in the original Greek language means "freedom." *Wow, God, you must be laughing now. What an amazing sense of humor*, I thought as I paid for my groceries. *Here I am set free by living in the unknown world that I can't see whereas before I was enslaved by living in the known world that I could see. God, you blow my mind!* I laughed.

Whether Mrs. Carmichael called and said yes to our renting or not, I knew my family and I were in God's will. Finally, I could be content right where God had me, or at least until the next step of faith would unfold.

Amazingly, this new faith journey was to become my daily routine. And just like God does, that very next day Mrs. Carmichael did indeed call and grant us a year lease on the house. God was right on time; that is His time; not mine. As we packed up from our beach rental, we were able to drive literally right down the street to the main road that encompassed the entire island and then turn right. There was our little yellow rental house! Since the island does not have street signs or street names, we quickly became known as "The Texans at the Yellow House."

That day we joyfully unloaded our three pallets of toys and luggage at our new home and were all ready to go! I'll admit it was somewhat anticlimactic; we did not have anything personal to add to the house. No framed family photographs, no wedding album on the coffee table, no soccer cleats by the front door. It seemed sort of lonely. *I guess God wants everything new,* I said trying to encourage myself. Outwardly I was already questioning this radical new beginning. Our house was cute but small; there was not much to it, three bedrooms and two bathrooms. But it was newly renovated, furnished and clean and it was ours to call "Home Sweet Home" for at least the next year.

* * * * * * *

I remembered scripture that was all about newness, then the Holy Spirit brought to mind the words in Isaiah 43:19, "I will make a way in the wilderness and rivers in the desert." Wasn't there something in the Word about "new"? It was easy to find my Bible since I only had a backpack of my essentials and it was right there on top. I opened to the verse in Revelation 21:5 which says, "Behold, I am making all things new." *Awesome God! And thank you so much!* I whispered to encourage myself.

As we wrapped up the move by unpacking our few belongings, we began talking together about how exciting it would be to attend the church we had found on our previous trip. Suddenly, a neighbor knocked on the door, stopping by with fresh avocados from their yard. The locals call them "pears" which was sort of confusing, but I was about to learn a lot of things were different; in fact, I would learn almost everything was entirely different about this island and community.

"Hello, I am Ms. Lucille and I live over yonder in the pink house with gray shutters," our new neighbor said.

After telling us a bit about her family, she said she had to leave to make her supper. As she left our house she casually mentioned, "Oh and don't forget to bring a dish to the supper social tomorrow."

"A dish?" I asked.

"You know a meat or a side for the meal we share after church," she replied.

"Oh, well, would it be okay if I made something my kids might like, such as spaghetti?"

She hesitated for a moment, smiled back and said, "Of course, darling."

Her thick accent was endearing and something I had to strain to understand. She spoke with a mixture of Britain's English and Bahamian English. It reminded me of an Australian accent too, but for the moment all those thoughts were put aside; I would need to run to what the locals called "the shop" to get my spaghetti ready for the following day.

As I raced out the door, I was surprised as I walked up to the grocery store to find a local woman locking the main entry doors. "What time do you close?" I asked.

"Oh 6, on Saturdays. Weekdays it's 5 and on Sundays, like everything else, we're closed."

"Um, well...." I murmured.

I guess she saw I was a little distraught because she quickly responded with an inviting smile, "What do ya need?"

"Well I was going to make spaghetti for the church social tomorrow, but I can see you are..."

"Oh, na problem, Darling. Let me just open on up and ya go get what you need," she smiled.

"Well thank you. And how will I pay you?"

"You just come by on Monday and we'll take care of it at my register. And by the way, I am Nelda."

"Hello Nelda, I'm Amy."

I gathered what I needed, said thank you and walked home to make my spaghetti.

"Michael, the locals are so nice. The store was closed but the cashier opened it for me, so I could get everything. Wasn't that nice? God's favor I would say."

"Yes, you're right, God's favor," Michael agreed.

And it was right then I knew I was exactly where we were supposed to be.

SECTION TWO

FREEDOM

For in Christ Jesus neither circumcision nor uncircumcision counts for anything, but only faith working through love.

Galatians 5:6

Chapter 6

Uncertainty –
What Trust Looks Like

Set your mind on the things above, not on the things that are on earth.

Colossians 3:2

"Amy, I didn't realize you brought supper for the church Sunday social. This is in a pastry dish." My face flushed red and I apologized to the elderly church lady, mumbling something about not knowing it was a cake dish. I was trying my best to become this excellent Proverbs 31 woman since God gave me a new perspective on life. *How is this going to happen, God? Time, Amy,* the Holy Spirit responded.

God had planted the idea in my heart of staying at home with my children and caring for my home, yet I had no idea how to do that. In my former life in Texas, I knew how to build a company and be a workaholic, but how to do this new thing God was asking was beyond me.

Through ample time God gave me the opportunity to try out this dream of godly womanhood in my new life. Our new church provided the class-room I needed. The life God was unfolding in this completely foreign environment was filled with women whose chief desire was exactly what I yearned for. By watching them, learning from them, and emulating them, I began to change. This process was difficult and slow because I was stub-born and independent. There were times of humiliation and rejection as "I" was no longer at the helm of my destiny and clearly in unfamiliar territory.

Yet, little by little, I would try new things in the kitchen. I was not about to quit, and my self-confidence began to grow. The change was hard; I was constantly harassed with doubt. Here I was again, chiding myself. "What do you know Amy? You brought spaghetti in a cake dish."

I felt discouraged and because of my pride my insecurity heightened.

I had made personal changes and choices, but our family faced bigger challenges. We were four and half months into our stay in the Bahamas and with no money left in the bank, pressure mounted. Bill collectors began calling and I was fearful. The money we had counted on from the sale of the speculative homes never came to fruition. What seemed like a lot of money from our moving sale had quickly run out. *How will we eat? What now Lord?* I asked in my prayers.

As Thanksgiving was quickly approaching, we were in a difficult situation. Typically, you cannot legally stay on extended vacations in the Bahamas, but we received an extension from the immigration office to do so. Once again God had us in the grips of His trust as we were able to stay but faced the grave situation of no work and no money. God's timing is always perfect, of course; just as I was thinking *"Well, we must go back home to live,"* He opened the only door we could see that had ministry potential. It was teaching English as a Second Language to Haitian adults.

An invitation had gone out at church to participate. We were aware of the many workers in the neighborhood, black men bent over, laboring in the yards, machetes in hand. But we had no idea they were not Bahamian but Haitian. It was only until we began to hear the locals say, "My Haitian," referring to a man or woman who worked for them, that we understood their social position within this society.

At about the same time, our Youth Pastor came to us and said, "You all should come to our Thanksgiving celebration at the church."

"Tell us about it."

"Our youth group puts it on for the Haitian church and Haitian community."

"Haitian community? Who are they?" I inquired.

"Oh, they are immigrants who live in the communities over the bridge. Usually, the youth and a few of our church members come out to support the event, so you and your family should come."

There it was again, *Haitians.* I wondered to myself why they were here in the Bahamas, but at the same time was thankful for the turkey dinner invitation.

We'd thought about a celebration of our own but could not afford to purchase a turkey to eat, as I discovered when I went shopping and told my husband what I found.

"$54 for a turkey?!" Michael said in disbelief.

"Yes, and that was the smallest *and* cheapest one," I replied.

I had learned very quickly that living on this island was expensive, especially the food. Everything was shipped into the Bahamas and most items were taxed 45% duty on top of the original price and freight. As we saw our bank account dwindle to nothing, we were desperate. We realized our hobby of fishing was no longer going to be a hobby but a life skill that allowed us to eat.

On past vacations, our family had enjoyed fishing in the Bahamas. Now looking back, it was easy to see that God used those times to knit our family together amid His glorious creation. When we were alone in the middle of the ocean, without phones or the internet and without our minds being centered on our business, we were focused on one another.

Here on Eleuthera we were grateful to have Michael's great fishing skills. Daily he and I would go out to secure our supper. We'd tuck our kids into bed, and quietly tip-toe out of the house, grab our fishing gear and plastic lawn chairs, walking a short block to the beach. Making ourselves at home we would cast our rods into the ocean and watch by the moonlight to see a fish swim up and swallow our bait. Whatever hooked the line was what we ate. Most of the time we caught gray snapper which was delicious white meat, but on occasion, we caught mutton snapper. Whatever God provided from his ocean was what we brought home to fillet for the following night's dinner.

When we told one of the locals how long we'd been doing that, he was astonished.

"85 days?!" You have got to be kidding! You have eaten fish that many days in a row?"

"Yes," I laughed.

I may have been laughing on the outside but on the inside, I was ashamed about our situation and doubted my decision to move and trust God. This was not at all what I had thought would happen when we moved to the Bahamas, nor what I thought things would look like. The glamorous island life I had envisioned was realistically filled with many unforeseen challenges as we would soon find out.

Another reminder of just how different things were from what I imagined was the daily task of doing laundry.

"I need more clothes pins, Michael."

My husband could see I was becoming a pro at double hanging shorts with only two pins, but the amount of laundry commanded more pins. Saving money was priority so I used anything I could to stretch the funds, like hanging the wash out to dry. As I stood outside in the scorching fall heat, I could not believe I had succumbed to a life of hand washing dishes and hanging clothes outside.

My mind went back to the house we had built and sold for ourselves in Texas. I saw myself standing in the backyard of the original house the day the sale closed. I was busy planning how, after I demolished the original house, I could use the footprint of the foundation to build a new, dream house for myself and family. I remembered being outside in the backyard, laughing at the old clothes line adjacent the house, thinking how antiquated and old fashion it was to wash and hang clothes.

I would never want to look out and see a clothes line as the view of my backyard, I had thought.

Then it hit me. God was saying, *look who's laughing now, Amy.*

It was at this moment I saw how entitled and arrogant my heart was and how I had not been thankful for the countless blessings God had bestowed on me in the U.S., how I had taken for granted the life he had given me in Texas.

Now here we were in stark contrast to my previous life. Island living was much more simplistic. In our new community, dishwashers were scarce in homes, dryers were too expensive to run, and air conditioning was a luxury. When our first electricity bill arrived in October, we were aghast at the $551 amount.

"How in the world can that be?" Michael asked. "We have a gas oven and a window unit in our bedroom that runs only at night only. And the electricity is only really the refrigerator and our day to day use. Plus, the kids are gone all day. Are you sure this is right, Amy?"

If the lack of cool air and high bills were not enough to discourage us, we became more downcast when we realized our local water presented problems. As the days went by, I saw white bleach spots on our colored shirts and begin to ask the locals, "What is going on with the water?"

"It's bleach" I was told. "The government puts bleach in the water to eliminate the disease."

"Oh, no," I thought. "Thank goodness we have not been drinking it," I told Michael.

58

City water was only used for bathing and cleaning, whereas drinking water was purchased.

Would brushing my teeth with the city water cause us to become sick? I wondered.

So many difficulties were hidden under the surface of daily life; everything required an adjustment. Outwardly our pristine community looked like the US, but now I was beginning to really understand what island living was all about; I was not at all certain I liked it. Other common island habits also became the norm for us. All four of our kids slept in our room at night on a futon mattress so that they could have the cold air from our window unit. When a child slept over, they joined the team and we became one very big happy family in our somewhat larger master bedroom. Intimacy between Michael and I became a luxury dedicated to the daytime hours now as we hibernated in the cold air-conditioned bedroom.

****

Yes, in a short amount of time God was working on me in grand ways. I knew this move was going to be life altering and that I was going to have to participate. From the beginning, I had asked God to show me how to have my identity in Him alone. I wanted peace and was willing to forego whatever He asked of me in order to have His fruit in my life. I wanted healing for my marriage and family and knew if God had given me His way, He was not going to let me down. His plan unfolded in all those repetitive days of fishing, when God gave Michael and I time to talk and reconnect with one another.

It was also during those days that I also was able to become a mother whose priority was her children. I relished teaching my three-year-old son preschool skills and in having short Bible studies ready for my kids when they came home at lunch. Baby steps towards a new life began to counter my fear as I grew with inward contentment and joy. God was working on every level in my life.

In the middle of our financial need, locals would randomly show up giving us fresh fruits or vegetables from their gardens, just like the neighbor who'd brought me that avocado. In this I saw hospitality, kindness, and generosity. And in the days after that first spaghetti meal, when I would forget things for recipes after the local supermarket had closed, I would ask a neighbor, "Can I borrow some butter?" and was never denied.

God was indeed changing me and developing me into the Proverbs 31 woman I always wanted to become, but the bigger battle was in my head; I had to let go. Let go of the past where I had built a successful company and reputation. Let go of being the author of my own destiny. How could I be a success if I constantly doubted God and this new life He was presenting? Although thankfulness abounded because I was being transformed along with my marriage, fear of God's provision still caused conflict and panic in my heart.

"Just have faith," my husband would say. "Amy, you must trust in God."

"But how, Michael?" I had no idea.

The enemy also taunted me with past clients who were still seeking our business for remodeling or home building in Texas. *Oh, Amy, you could fly back and forth,* the Devil would whisper in my ear. *That is what a Proverbs 31 woman would do. She cares well for her household. Don't you know that's what it says?* The struggle was real.

I would succumb to doubt, asking God, *how can I believe You when we have no idea what we are doing and how we are going to live?* Frantic pleas for relief and answers were made but God answered in an unexpected way. *Gratitude, Amy. Come to me with gratitude,* I heard him say. Searching scripture, I found some of my favorite verses from Philippians 4: 6–7 and began to say it out loud "...do not be anxious about anything, but in everything by prayer and supplication with thanksgiving let your requests be known to God. And the peace of God, which surpasses all understanding, will guard your hearts and minds in Christ Jesus."

Slowly God was teaching me to be thankful for anything and everything with a heart of appreciation. I learned very quickly that I better obey Him; it was sink or swim. Dire times required dire measures and almost overnight I employed my new gratitude campaign. Reversing my thinking by saying things like, "I have clothes without bleach on them today!" caused me to rejoice. I now began to look for anything I could be thankful for and slowly day by day we were making it. Making it and enjoying our newfound island life. The peace had begun, but some days held more victory than others. My constant flip-flopping mindset was a hurdle I had to overcome and soon so that I could keep my sanity.

In the weeks that lead up to the Thanksgiving dinner, I pressed into God's new way for me daily. While I did so, I began to search for His voice in every detail as He had begun to teach me. I knew He would not leave me or forsake me and the only way I could maintain this peace was to change my thinking about this new life He was unfolding.

"Please, Lord, help me change." I prayed one night. Amazingly, that was the very thing He was doing in my heart, yet I mistakenly did not realize the sorrow and pain I was experiencing was more layers God was peeling away so I could become the woman He already knew I was. It was only in my weakness that His strength could cause the light to come in and expose truths I needed, quenching my thirsty soul.

Chapter 7

Confirmation – Home Sweet Home

The Lord will fulfill his purpose for me; your steadfast love, O LORD, endures forever. Do not forsake the work of your hands.

Psalm 138:8

As the ferry pulled away for the dock I sat firmly anchored in the back of the boat where breezes gently blew, water spewing from the engine. A rainbow appeared low in the water just as the engine kicked up a notch. *Oh Lord, is that a good sign of covenant keeping commitment from you? Maybe you are reassuring me it is your will for us to live here forever? Oh, please allow this appointment to go well so we can stay in the Bahamas.*

Although we had been given an additional time to reside in the Bahamas upon our arrival, we'd now been told by the lead Immigration Officer in our area that we had to apply to the Chief Officer of Immigration for the island of Eleuthera for permission to stay. The office was far away in a small town called Governor's Harbor, and it would require a lot of effort to get there since we did not have any transportation.

This meeting was urgent. I replayed the conversation from the day before, Ms. Deveaux, the Regional Immigration Officer, had scolded us, "You cannot remain in the country, you must leave immediately."

The stern look in her eyes was unforgiving.

"But we had no idea Ms. Deveaux. We have been given an extension," I stammered, tears welling up in my eyes.

"The children may not attend school. This is unheard of and I still cannot fathom how they are attending," she continued.

She may not have known how, but God did. He alone had given us favor with the local government when we first arrived. It was in August just days after our arrival, that I learned we must be approved by the top local authority to do anything in our community of Spanish Wells. Even though the school principal had given us verbal approval over the phone three months prior, I was beginning to understand that the town's motto of "Come visit, but don't try to change us," was going to be enforced if we challenged it. It was quickly becoming apparent what it was like being an outsider on an island of generational families. I decided in that first interview with the local Chief Councilor I was not about to rock the boat with Mr. Rolle, the salty yet savvy gentleman with whom I was speaking.

As the conversation began, I wanted to point out to him that the Bahamian government's website showed we should be allowed to stay for eight months legally. I quickly surmised from his charming and curious demeanor that it would be best to answer his questions politely giving him the utmost respect. He periodically interrupted our conversation, taking big puffs from the cigarette dangling from his mouth, all the while yelling answers back to his secretary from questions she was shouting from the front office. This man was obviously busy; everyone came to see him if they needed something.

"Who do ya say ya know?" Mr. Rolle asked.

Discerning the answer to this question was of utmost importance. I paused before I answered, "Darcie and Tim Thompson." I knew the residents operated the town on a first name basis. Thankfully, I had already gleaned from the Thompsons, our only Bahamian friends whom we'd met on our first vacation to Spanish Wells, that there are three predominant families on the island. The Thompsons were one of them. This obviously carried some sort of weight with Mr. Rolle.

"Um, well," he mumbled as the end of his cigarette ashes almost fell on his desk, "Let me check into a few things and get back to you." He didn't seem to mind that the ashes were now all over the paperwork on his cluttered desk.

Three agonizing days later, we received a phone call from the School Principal saying the children had been approved to attend school. All of this was quite shocking to us because supposedly we had already been cleared when I had spoken to her during that initial phone interview. I was beginning to see that God alone would "open to us a door" as Colossians 4:3 says. It was becoming obvious this close-knit community did not readily accept strangers. Clearly God was working through people and allowing us to stay, confirming His plan and His will for our family.

Now we had found ourselves up against a wall with Ms. Deveaux. Finally, after much pleading and apologizing, she relented, and our unspoken prayers were answered. However, instead of giving us permission to stay, she insisted that she would now defer the decision to the highest person in the office of Immigration on the entire island. That meeting was to happen the following day and in another city on the island. So here we were on our way to meet Ms. Deveaux's boss, the Chief Immigration Officer of the island of Eleuthera.

After all of this I was beginning to see that our journey was much like the Apostle Paul's as he was sent from King to King to await his fate of life or death. Thankfully, we were not being crucified *yet*, but we were learning exactly what it looked like to die daily to our plans and become fully surrendered to God's unfolding path.

* * * * * * *

After we got off the boat, we picked up a rental car and drove the hour and half to meet the Officer in Governor's Harbor. Not much was said as Michael and I prayed the whole way, but the peace God gave us that morning instilled confidence that if God did indeed want us to stay, He would continue to provide the way. We were reminded of Ephesians 1: 11, "In him we were also chosen, having been predestined according to the plan of him who works out everything in conformity with the purpose of his will."

"Michael, did you see the rainbow on our ferry ride?" I asked.

"No," he replied.

"I think God is saying it's going to be ok."

"I know it will."

Once again Michael's faith far outweighed mine and I was glad to rely on his confidence.

When we arrived at the Immigration building, we waited for a very long time until our paperwork was reviewed. Finally, we were escorted back to an office. After we sat down with a Mrs. Higgs, she asked, "Mrs. Boykin, exactly what are you doing here in the Bahamas?"

I was surprised by the directness of her question and wondered why she was addressing me and not Michael. Somehow God gave me the ability to speak what sounded to me like a crazy response.

"Mrs. Higgs, we are not quite sure. My family and I have been coming to the Bahamas for years and God spoke to us and told us to move here. That was in 2006. Finally, we did move here last August. We sold everything we owned in Texas, closed our company and we are now waiting for God to show us what to do. We know He wants us to do something in ministry and we are attending the local church in Spanish Wells and serving by teaching English to the Haitian adults."

Without blinking, Mrs. Higgs glared at Michael and I after I had finished speaking. It was not a comforting look but the kind that sizes you up and peers directly into your soul.

I held my breath as her dark brown eyes held my attention, awaiting her response of rejection. She just continued to look at us for what seemed like eternity. Then, as if what I had said was something she heard every day, she responded. "Well, Mr. and Mrs. Boykin, if you will get these other necessary documents I need, I will submit your paperwork to Nassau for approval."

Time stood still, I was stunned. *Approval?* I thought to myself. *What? Did I hear her correctly?* Inwardly I was jumping for joy, I wanted to give everyone high fives and whoop and holler but thank goodness, I kept my cool. Instead, Michael and I shook her hand goodbye and she quickly ushered us out. Michael told her we would love to bring her some fish the next time we saw her. God was clearly in control of our destiny and relief washed over me as we thanked her. We walked to our rental car to head home.

As Michael and I joyfully celebrated our leap over this hurdle we knew we still were living in uncertainty, but at least we were one step closer to whatever God intended. As we arrived at our children's school to pick them up, they ran over excitedly.

"Mom are they going to let us stay?" Marley inquired.

We had no idea our four children also were feeling anxious about our future until the onset of questions started coming. As we drove up to our little yellow house, more questions came, "What did they say?" "Will we have to leave?" "Where will we go?"

I could tell by the questions my children had been plagued with silent doubt. Reassuring them, Michael and I told them God had provided the way for us to remain in the Bahamas. At dinner that night we sat around the table and opened the Bible to 1 John 5:14–15, "And this is the confidence that we have toward him, that if we ask anything according to his will he hears us. And if we know that he hears us in whatever we ask, we know that we have the requests that we have asked him."

Michael went on to thank the Lord for answering our prayer and giving us victory in His plan for our family. Tearfully we all relished in God's goodness and felt relief that we indeed were on the right course. Little James jumped up from his chair and shouted, "Does this mean I am Bahamian now?" We all laughed but I thought it too complicated to explain that we now understood as a family where our true citizenship was. It would never again be a nationality but a state of the heart as a follower of Christ.

As Fall of 2010 progressed, we settled into our new life. Everything was completely different from the U.S. Although our community is predominantly white, which is unusual for the Bahamas since it is a black nation, hardly anything resembled our former life. We were quickly learning that the U.S. was an idol for this community. The American dream and U.S. lifestyle were what they aspired towards.

In direct contrast to the Bahamian mindset, God began to show us clearly that you can't live a divided life. "Do not love the world or anything of the world," stood out from Scripture in 1 John 2:15. As we learned about our new neighborhood, we were thankful God had plucked us from the idol worshipping lifestyle in the US.

We enjoyed being part of a community where church was the center of life. Most locals attended both Sunday morning and evening. In fact, it was the expected norm to be at both services. Church was also held one other night during the week. Back at home in Texas, we did attend church regularly, but it was just another event we had each week, sandwiched next to tennis lessons, baseball practice, business meetings, PTA and football games.

The priority that Christianity had in the lives of the Bahamian people was evident. We were beginning to understand since the Bahamas calls itself a Christian nation, the church had prominence in all areas of the community even in governmental affairs unlike in the U.S. At school, local meetings and gatherings the ceremonies always included an opening and closing prayer; in fact, it was expected as part of routine protocol. People spoke about Jesus, Christianity and religion regularly and church *seemed* to be at the center of most locals' lives, but they did not recognize this ideology because they had grown up in it. They did not realize what a gift it was for them to be in a Christ-centered nation.

All of this became crystal clear one night at dinner. We had been asked by our friends the Thompsons to meet for supper at the local restaurant. Quickly I had said "Yes", grateful for the invitation and a new dinner option. Anything but fish would be a welcome change. Darcie had been the first person I met when we attended the local church that first vacation we took over a year ago on the island. Since that meeting in the church nursery, she and I had become good friends and now we were getting our husbands to become better friends, too.

"Why do you want to live here? You won't last a year," Tim said.

Michael and I looked at each other, puzzled.

"There is nothing to do here," Darcie said in a sarcastic, laughing way, nodding her head at Tim. I could tell by their body language they were confident we would be bored in the Bahamas and leave soon.

If their "nothing" meant no movie theaters, social events, sporting events, and anything else you can imagine the U.S. fills its time with that was true. There was plenty "to do," with a Methodist church, a Brethren church and a non-denominational church having a youth group or service every night of the week except Saturday. For a small island to have three churches seemed like quite a lot to us and obviously showed the place church had in the lives of the islanders.

What Tim and Darcie did not understand was the simplicity of life with Christ, that He was teaching us He alone would be the focus of our family. Coming to the feast with Jesus was our nourishment.

"You don't understand, Tim. The U.S. for us was full of distractions. Whether it's an after-school practice for one of our four kids' sports, playing video games or wasting time watching TV, we've found it very different here. There is a real peace living on this undiscovered, simple island. Everything is slow-paced, and we love it."

"Did you know that in the US people are glued to their phones and social media?" I added.

"Even our kids had iPods before they came and were constantly listening to music. Here, we don't even see cellular phones, in fact, I don't think anyone's discovered them or social media!"

"We love that we can sit down at dinner every night as a family and read the Bible together. We love that the town shuts down for lunch from 12 to 1 and we pick up our kids from school to eat together. We love that we can go to church every night if we want and learn about Jesus. That watching the sunset is our nightly 'to do' while we watch our kids run races on the beach racing, singing and dancing."

We had imagined our new haven of the Bahamas was much like what we had been taught in elementary school History classes about the U.S. in the 1950's. This proved to be true; the comparisons were similar. God in His glorious way had sent us to His little slice of heaven on earth and we were thankful. Romans 1:20 says, "For his invisible attributes, namely, his eternal power and divine nature, have been perceived, ever since the creation of the world, in the things that have been made…"

Yes, we reveled in God's creation in the Bahamas.

* * * * * * *

With our paperwork to reside in the Bahamas submitted, the kids in school and friendships forming, we began to settle into our new Bahamian life. Other regular routines emerged as well such as fishing and farming. Now with plenty of time on my hands, I had a garden and grew vegetables of all sorts. Soon Michael joined in by catching wild chickens and tending to them. God was shaping our life into what He envisioned.

If we truly were going to be Jesus' pupils, we had to obey the Teacher. Day by day He renewed our strength to obey Him and learn from Him. Romans 12:1 was now our life principle, "I appeal to you therefore, brothers, by the mercies of God, to present your bodies as a living sacrifice, holy and acceptable to God, which is your spiritual worship."

My daily sacrifice was to say "no" to me and "yes" to He. To look like Him was to become more holy. Only by His mercy was I able to change into God's image-bearer. As I became more like Jesus, I worshipped Him. Knowing Him through the Bible changed me and gave me His viewpoint. I was beginning to understand my "worship" meant I was to do everything for Him and His glory. This process would continually change me to look more and more like Jesus. The only way to do this was to practice living out Scripture and live centered in love. Indeed, Jesus was the "more" that I needed. He had given my family and I a new beginning; one that we could have never envisioned with Him at the helm.

With God fully anchored in my heart as number one, I now had peace in the foundation He was laying and prayed for confidence to look ahead to His plan. *Please Lord, give me stability knowing You will continue to provide for my family Your way in every aspect of our lives;* I would pray, *Please, Lord, please.*

What I did not realize is He already had, and that security was being the peace of knowing and being "in Christ" alone.

Chapter 8

A New Beginning

*Then Peter said to Him, "Behold, we have
left everything and followed You; what then will
there be for us?"*

Matthew 19:27

Running along the two-and-a-half-mile beach of our new island I watched the clouds roll in. The gorgeous dark gray sky starkly contrasted with the soft, light aqua water. As the storm approached, the entire picture was overcast with gloom and doom. Lightning shrieked against the now charcoal sky and I quickly jetted for the only shelter I could find on the beach. A dilapidated building was my refuge from the storm, literally and figuratively. I was crying to the point of choking. The downpour of rain, the thunder and lightning, all expressed exactly how I felt as I issued a downpour of my own, flooding the sand with my tears, huffing and puffing to catch my breath between sobs. Everything about the scene reflected how I felt-forlorn and dejected. The silence was broken by an almost audible voice, "Let me do it, Amy," God said. I heard Him answer my prayer even though I hadn't said a word.

I thought of David's words in Psalm 139 in verses 1–7, "O LORD, you have searched me and known me! You know when I sit down and when I rise up; You understand my thoughts from afar. You search out my path and my lying down; You are aware of all my ways. Even before a word is on my tongue, You know all about it. You hem me in behind and before; You have laid Your hand upon me. Such knowledge is too wonderful for me, too lofty for me to attain. Where shall I go to escape Your Spirit? Where can I flee from Your presence?"

God was always with me. I whispered. *Did I know that? Did I believe it? Did I realize God knew my heart before I even knew it?* He was answering unspoken prayers.

Since that initial call of, "Move to the Bahamas," God was now giving me the call to the next chapter of my life, a life anchored in faith.

"Rest and trust, Amy. I *will* sustain you," I heard Him say.

Amazing, that was really God, I said to myself. Although I was trying to focus on my newfound gratitude strategy, double-mindedness had persisted, and inner turmoil remained. I would not fully give in to God's new life for me. I was struggling to see how to ascribe God's character and nature to my life and become that new woman He was telling me I already was. Some days I had more victory than others, but on this day, I felt I was at my breaking point until I'd heard God's clear voice. *Was that really the Holy Spirit?* I thought. Yes, it was. Sitting on the bench in a dilapidated shack God said it again, "Let me do it. Rest and trust, Amy. I will sustain you."

But how God? How?

As the rain subsided, I heard nothing else but silence. After what seemed like a long time of staring at the wet sand and beautiful ocean, I began to feel comfort and peace, the very words I had heard resonated throughout my entire being. Relieved and quieted, I mustered up the strength to run home. As the storm had passed, so too had the 'storm' of my pity party. I jogged home slowly, trying to process what God meant by these words.

The answer came that next morning as I unpacked a small surprise package my sister had tucked away in our pallet from Texas. I opened the padded envelope and saw a book with two DVDs. "Never Give Up" by Joyce Meyer was the title on the cover. *Okay, Lord this must be from You.*

I began to listen and read, answering the workbook questions that accompanied the DVD. I realized I had never used scripture as the foundation for my life. It seemed so basic, but I had never been taught that there was power in speaking the promises in the Bible. Speaking the Word of God birthed His truth into existence. I recollected Hebrews 4:12 which says, "For the word of God is alive and active. Sharper than any double-edged sword, it penetrates even to dividing soul and spirit, joint and marrow; it judges the thoughts, and attitudes of the heart." I searched for other scripture confirming this idea. One verse was Isaiah 55:11, "...so shall my word be that goes out from my mouth; it shall not return empty, but it shall accomplish that which I purpose, and shall succeed in the thing for which I sent it." Piecing what I knew together like a puzzle I now understood if I have Jesus indwelling me through the Holy Spirit, I had the power to speak scripture and birth it.

Even though I knew scripture, went to Bible studies, and led them in high school, attended small group and prayed and journaled daily, I had never memorized scripture and used it as the principle by which I lived. I continued to dive into this study and saw that my mind was the battleground for Satan and God. Although I called myself a Christian, I had lived a life based on the world's view of what I had been taught in school and my upbringing and filtered my life through my worldly viewpoint, not the Bible.

THE WAY

God was teaching me His view is very different. Based solely on His word was to apply these truths by living them out. If I was to believe in Him, I had to obey Him.

One key scripture that opened my heart to this concept was from John 14:26, "But the Helper, the Holy Spirit, whom the Father will send in my name, he will teach you all things and bring to remembrance all that I have said to you." God, through the power of the Holy Spirit, was opening my mind to understanding Him as I learned and applied his Word to my life daily. Now Scriptures like, "He who has My commandments and keeps them is the one who loves Me; and he who loves Me will be loved by My Father, and I will love him and will disclose Myself to him," (John 14:21) meant something. The Holy Spirit was real, not a mystical thing or "it" but the third person of the Trinity that I could now trust. I could know Him because Jesus imparted Him to me when I walked in faithful obedience to His word.

More obedience was to come, but I had to know and renew my mind through scripture day by day. I had to begin to understand how to be who God says I am from His Word and believe it. Weekly God would show me a problem area in my life and then I would find scripture that addressed the issue. For example, to fight my fears I memorized scripture like Joshua 1:9, "Have I not commanded you? Be strong and courageous. Do not be afraid; do not be discouraged, for the LORD, your God is with you wherever you go."

I would say this aloud and to myself when fears arose during very practical circumstances, like when Michael and I would fight over our unknown day to day survival. I used my morning runs as my time to memorize scripture by carrying little sticky notes with verses on them. I would sing familiar tunes like "Mary had a little lamb" but replace the words in the song with words from a Scripture to help me remember it. Although I always enjoyed running, now I longed for my runs with God and during them, He changed my thinking. He replaced my thoughts with His thoughts and my ways with His ways.

For the first time in my life, I could sense a peace that was replacing an emptiness I didn't know was there. Even after years of claiming Jesus as my Savior, a new biblical foundation was growing exponentially. And just as inwardly I was being renewed, outwardly my marriage was also

74

changing into one where we, as a couple, were united in our understanding that God would supply all our needs. Instead of looking to each other to meet desires and longings, Michael and I began a new chapter in our marriage reading the Bible together, praying together and fasting together. God was focusing on who we each were in Jesus and creating a framework cemented in Him alone.

I began to see that Michael could never meet my needs like God. That he and I were both continuously being refined and it was in the purging of our bad habits that we became more like Jesus. Michael sanctified me, and I sanctified him. Marriage was created for this reason to sanctify each other with Christ at our center. The false idea I had been raised to believe of attaining perfection for not only my marriage but for myself was unrealistic, as God alone is only perfect. I needed to trust Him for this reason. Jesus took my place and my sin so that I could through my God-given free will pursue a life with Him and for Him. My identity was blossoming because of this firm foundation with the grace of Jesus as my justification.

As my mind opened up, God expanded his teaching by showing me and Michael the difference between "needs" and "wants," too. Slowly, as a couple, we began to live with thankfulness at the slightest provision from God. People would unexpectedly drop lobster off at our house. Strangers giving us $100 showed God's many ways of seeing our needs and providing for us as Philippians 4:19 says, "And my God will supply every need of yours according to His riches in glory in Christ Jesus."

Gradually, God was unfolding a life based solely on the Bible. By studying God's word, meditating on it and applying it I was changing. I saw how my former life was lived in shades of gray whereas the Bible addressed specific ways to live life. I was beginning to understand that Scripture has power as 2 Timothy 3:16–17 relates, "All scripture is breathed out by God and profitable for teaching, for reproof, for correction, and for training in righteousness, that the man of God may be competent, equipped for every good work."

I also discovered that scripture is truth to be believed and lived out as John 16:13–15 says, "When the Spirit of truth comes, he will guide you into all the truth, for he will not speak on his own authority, but whatever he hears he will speak, and he will declare to you the things that are to come. He will glorify me, for he will take what is mine and declare it to you. All that the Father has is mine; therefore, I said that he will take what is mine and declare it to you."

This Scripture correlates to the power of the Holy Spirit, "But, the anointing which you received from him abides in you, and you have no need for anyone to teach you. But as his anointing teaches you about everything, and is true, and is no lie- just as it has taught you, you abide in him." (1 John 2:27.)

As I continued to pray, the Holy Spirit reminded me about man being likened to a clay pot. Jeremiah 18:3–4 summarizes God's authority over man this way, "So I went down to the potter's house and saw him working at the wheel. But the pot he was shaping from the clay was marred in his hands, so the potter formed it into another pot, shaping it as seemed best to him." I realized that God, "the potter," had shattered my first life, just as in the imagery of the clay pot. Now He was remolding me into that clay He envisioned. My very existence in Him was unfolding before my eyes. I prayed, *Lord, please help me to not live by my own strength and become the woman You envision. Let this be my new beginning. In your name I pray, amen.*

Chapter 9

Meeting Our Neighbors – Changing Us from the Inside Out

And we all, who with unveiled faces contemplate the Lord's glory, are being transformed into his image with ever-increasing glory, which comes from the Lord, who is the Spirit.

2 Corinthians 3:18

THE WAY

The Thanksgiving Day gathering was finally here. As we pulled our golf cart into the church parking lot that evening, God's new way was about to be unfolded in our lives. There was a plethora of tables and chairs set up, yet most were empty. It looked like mostly young teens and children in attendance and I could tell from their clothes these Haitian guests had tried to dress in their best attire. What struck me about the scene was the separation of local Bahamian people from the Haitian people. There were only a few members from our congregation in attendance, except for the church Youth group which was hosting the event. As I mingled with the crowd, we saw the Youth Pastor, Matthew.

"Come on in and grab a chair!" he hollered.

Before I could even head into Fellowship Hall to fix my supper plate, I saw three black girls laughing and hugging one another out of the corner of my eye.

Drawn by their infectious joy, I walked over and introduced myself. "Hi, I'm Amy. What are your names?"

The first to respond boldly said, "Good evening, my name is Suzelynda."

She had a big puffy afro and a beautiful smile.

"Oh, what a lovely name," I replied.

After meeting the three girls, Suzelynda stepped forward and asked, "Would you take our photo?"

I had my camera casually swung around my shoulder with the intention of taking a Thanksgiving picture of my family but was happy to take a photo of these young girls. After dinner I told them I would make them each a copy and bring it to them. With not much else to say, they scurried off laughing. Suzelynda's personality left a strong impression. She was different from what my daughter Marley had told me about how Haitian girls usually behave around people.

'Mom, women are treated like they are they 'less than,' Marley said.

"What do you mean?" I replied.

"Well at school, none of the girls look you in the eye."

78

I began to notice this when I picked up our kids from school. The girls all looked down at the ground whenever I casually said "Hello." Yet here was this vibrant girl, Suzelynda, full of life who'd looked me directly in the eyes and asked me to take her picture. I liked her confidence; she obviously was a leader. Her fearless smile with her perfectly straight, white teeth lit up her whole countenance, a stark contrast against her dark, ebony-colored skin.

"Yes, this girl has something special," I thought as my camera clicked away.

* * * * * * *

The holidays were over and when school started back after Christmas break, I was anxious to find the young Haitian girls I had met some five weeks prior.

I thought our youth leader Matthew might know.

"Where can I find the Haitian communities you told us about?" I asked him.

"Well, there are three areas they live in, but I would start at the one where the Pastor lives. It is called "Apea." "You can find it easily as you go over the bridge; it's the street on the right and a way down on the right."

"Okay, thanks." I replied. I quickly went off to find this Apea neighborhood and the girls.

When I arrived, I was surprised by what I saw. Tiny houses no bigger than the size of an American bedroom were interconnected to one another with narrow walkways between them. A woman was sitting outside cooking on an open fire in a tiny passageway. Roosters were running around, and flies were swarming above heaps of trash piled at the front of the community. Only women sat outside, and I watched curiously as they hand washed clothes in big, round metal bins.

When I asked, they did not really understand my question about locating the girls since they spoke Creole and not English. I went back home, my mind full of questions about these people, their way of life and living conditions.

THE WAY

My only experience with this kind of poverty was back home in Texas when our church small group had supported a homeless woman and the community where she lived. We had an annual Thanksgiving supper for her and all the other homeless people who lived in East Austin, considered a bad part of town. Our group would purchase and distribute gifts to the community for Christmas, but that was the limit of my experience. What I had seen in Apea far exceeded the poor conditions I had witnessed in Austin.

I decided to check in with daughter Marley again; maybe she would know where the girls lived. "Marley, where do you think I can find the girls we met at the Thanksgiving dinner?" Marley was outgoing and unafraid, so I knew she would be the one to ask.

"Mom, I don't know which grade they are in, but they're probably at the picnic tables at school during lunch." "Marley, but we come home for lunch. Remember? School doesn't have a cafeteria, and everyone gets picked up and goes home, sweetheart."

"No, Mom, the Haitian kids don't have transportation, they stay at school."

"I don't think they even have lunch," Josie chimed in.

"No lunch?" I said.

"Yeah, I heard they only eat one meal a day which is usually bread with peanut butter or maybe spaghetti noodles with ketchup." Marley added.

How in the world could this be? I thought to myself. *The people in this community must know about this,* I wondered. *And if they do, why aren't they helping these children? If this is true Lord,* I prayed, *please show me how to help these children in need.* I had seen some of the locals helping by employing the Haitian people, but not very many.

I went looking for a verse in the Bible I knew addressed something about refugees. I found it in Leviticus 19:33–34 "When a stranger sojourns with you in your land, you shall not do him wrong. You shall treat the stranger who sojourns with you as the native among you, and you shall love him as yourself, for you were strangers in the land of Egypt: I am the Lord your God."

Lord, let me help them, if it is your will for me, I prayed confidently.

* * * * * * *

For the time being that prayer would be unanswered as we struggled to provide daily meals for our own family; we too were sojourners in this country. I continued my mission to find the girls to at least give them the promised picture I had taken over Thanksgiving. One day as school let out, I watched as kids exited and saw one of the other girls who had been with Suzelynda. Quickly I jumped out of my golf cart and stopped her.

"Hi, excuse me. Do you remember me? I took this picture of you and your friends at the Thanksgiving dinner at the church."

"Oh yes," she replied. "Thank you."

I handed her the picture and went on to ask, "Where are the other girls so I can give them their copy?"

"Oh, one is over there but the other is gone."

"Oh, okay, thank you. Um, but what do you mean 'gone'?"

"Oh, she's in jail or something."

My heart sank as I saw the other girl cross over to me. As I handed the second girl the picture, I remember the girl who was missing…. *Suzelynda!*

Heartbroken because of the beautiful impression this girl had made on me, I wondered what had happened to cause her to go to jail. I prayed, *Oh Lord, please help me find her if it is your will.* Our new island was safe, and I had never heard of anyone going to jail. It did not make sense.

Over the course of that week, as I pondered how to look for more details about this teenage girl, I became distracted with our English class preparations. Michael and I would be teaching the beginners class of English to the Haitian adults as our lives were being shifted to this newfound calling. Since neither of us were teachers we had to teach ourselves how to teach. Lots of time and energy went into developing lesson plans and alphabet cards so that we could hold our bi-weekly classes.

I realized little by little God was not only providing for our family but showing me we were living out this Scripture, "Do not merely listen to the word, and so deceive yourselves. Do what it says." (James 1: 22.) Yes, miraculously we found ourselves 'doing ministry' as Michael and I taught the Haitian adults English and our children taught the Haitian children English. The kids also helped with homework at the same time. It was a beautiful beginning to this new work God was birthing.

We were also ministering to ourselves by becoming a Christ-centered family, focusing on what it meant to live out the Bible. Nightly dinner time devotions, prayer and serving were an expression of God's work in our lives. At our church we were growing too, by being taught great foundational truths about Christ alone. Now we were changing from the inside out, being transformed from the world instead of conformed to it. God afforded us this time of renewal and allowed us to learn about love and how to love. Love Him first so we could in turn love each other and other people, such as our new local Bahamian friends, others such as our own children and extended family, and others such as beloved Haitian sojourners. God was graciously changing our hearts of stone and turning them into hearts of flesh.

The familiar Sunday school song, "Red or yellow, black or white, they are precious in His sight. Jesus loves the little children of the world," was a real heart condition now.

God also did an amazing thing during this time by providing for us financially. At the beginning of 2011 we remembered we had some items still in a small storage unit that might be worth some money. Thankfully, family living back in Texas helped us by getting these items and selling them. Weekly we would have something to sell, like an anniversary present of custom-made boots I had given my husband which were sold for twenty-five hundred dollars. Other items such as antique guns and rifles Michael had kept in hopes of teaching our kids to hunt someday gave us eleven hundred dollars overnight! Relief was abounding! And just like that God multiplied the loaves and fish. He now satisfied and nourished us by multiplying our little into a lot, and somehow by His way we were surviving.

We did not have anything to spare but we had exactly what we needed to live. God taught us how to live joyfully like He says in 1 Timothy 6:8, "But if we have food and clothing, with these things we will be content." With this new mindset our family trusted God daily. Although God was meeting our needs inside, I prayerfully hoped God would give me some sort of security as to what our future held.

Little did I know at this time, but God was adjusting my perspective that there isn't anything permanent about this life on earth and I would never find true contentment until I embraced this truth. The "sustaining" God had spoken to me on that run in the rain months before would last a lifetime. My true citizenship would not come until He someday brought me home to be with Him in heaven. *Could I maintain peace and live by joy, really?* I wondered, hoped and prayed.

Chapter 10

Helping a Hidden Community-God's Fullness

And the King will answer them, Truly, I say to you,
as you did it to one of the least of these my brothers,
you did it to me.

Matthew 25:40

"A", not "I" Gesner; "A" like "Adam" in the Bible.

"J!" Michael called out the next letter. "J is for Jezi or Jesus in English." Michael said.

Suddenly Evans' hand shot up in the air, "INGO!" he said.

Michael laughed and said, "Ok great, but it's "BINGO," Evans not "INGO!" You won!"

Two years into teaching English as a Second Language to the Haitian adults, Michael and I had found great ways to teach the Bible and English using American games like Bingo. We were building friendships and looked forward to our teaching times and fellowship. It was during these classes that we forged relationships and learned about Haitian culture and life. We learned that most of the Haitian people had come to the Bahamas for a better life, many of them willing to risk everything by coming on small boats from Haiti. There were often reports in the local paper of boats wrecking and bodies discovered eaten by sharks.

As our friendships grew, we saw the discrepancy in living life as a Christian yet not helping the people right before us who are the "least of these." Our new friends were humble and in need. As we got to know them better, we would go into Apea, the area where most of the Haitian population lived, and spend time with them. Helping them became a top priority for us. With non-drinkable water and cooking over open fires, even the basics of daily existence were hard. But it was also hard for the Bahamians. The continuing US recession directly affected our small island. With little work for the Bahamians there was even less for the Haitians. This fact coupled with their struggle to provide for their families was evident from all that we saw.

As my daughter Marley had pointed out a year earlier, she was correct that most of the Haitians only ate one meal a day. Upon one visit to see a family with children, I was startled when I saw a group of girls giggling as they leaned over and were spitting what looked like white toothpaste from their mouths onto the ground some distance beneath them.

"Sankeisha, I am so sorry, I did not know you girls were here. I've never walked to the back of your house and didn't know this was a private area where you bathed."

"Oh, good morning Ms. Amy" she replied. "It's okay."

"What are you doing?" I asked.

"I brushin my teeth," she replied smiling.

"How? Is that water in the bucket?" I asked.

"Yes. I go down to the sea to get the water in this bucket and bathe with it too."

I turned to the girl beside her. "Oh, is that what you are doing, Roseline?"

Roseline was also standing on the concrete stoop using a sponge and soap, washing her face and arm pits. I felt embarrassed and stared down at the ground as these girls were getting ready for the day right out in the open. On one hand, I was glad they were comfortable enough around me to not be affected by my surprise appearance. On the other hand, I was saddened by the realization that it was normal for these girls to bathe like this-outside in the open air-for all to see. I realized the incredible blessing God had given me by the simple fact that our family had a bathroom and a bedroom. *Oh Lord, how incredibly selfish I am.*

Bathrooms were indeed uncommon in the Apea community; people were using the local water or even the salty sea water for bathing and washing, just like Sankeisha and Roseline. This practice led to many health problems within the community and I now understood the reason behind the constant sickness in the Haitian community.

As I excused myself, I walked through the tiny walkways that meandered between the houses back to my golf cart. There was Sankeisha's mom cooking on an open fire in the middle of one of the small corridors.

"Stephanie, what are you cooking? It smells so good. And hey, Ricardo, what are you up to?"

Sankeisha's little brother was right there helping grind up spices in a wooden bowl with a wooden mallet.

I didn't realize Sankeisha had followed me until she translated her mother's response to my question from Creole to English.

"Ms. Amy, I don't know what you would call this dish in English, but it is pork. We call it *griole*. My Mom wants me to make you a plate."

"Oh no, please save it for yourself. I am just fine but thank you."

Walking away, I saw the stark contrast of the local Bahamian lifestyle to the Haitian living conditions. *Why were more locals not helping?* I wondered.

While I pondered why my Bahamian neighbors were not assisting the Haitian community, it did not stop me from trying to address these needs myself. Michael would regularly donate extra fish he caught to them. Any extra food or clothing we had we gave away. Since my children attended the local school, I also got to know the Haitian children who attended school with them. I quickly learned that most of these Haitian children were significantly behind in school work. Now I could see why as we were teaching the adults; few could read or write English well. Creole was the predominant language of this first generation of Haitian adults residing in the Bahamas, so few of these parents could help with school work. No wonder their children were being left behind. Far behind. Most of the children repeated grades for two to three years.

This situation gave me the idea to begin tutoring Haitian children of all ages, so I enlisted my family to help. We began by asking the school principal if we could tutor the students that needed it.

"Mrs. Sweeting, it seems to me that you have an issue with the Haitian children being so far behind in school. May I start an after-school program to help them?"

"Mrs. Boykin, let me think about it."

Days passed by without a response and then one day she called me.

"Mrs. Boykin, I will allow a class, but I will first send home a note to the parents requesting a meeting with their consent on a written permission slip."

As I anxiously awaited the final approval I jumped for joy. Finally, a week and a half later I received word from Mrs. Sweeting that the parent response had been overwhelming. Every grade was requesting assistance but at this time she only wanted to proceed with the Primary school students in grades 1 to 6. I, too, was overwhelmed. God was growing His plan, but I would need help! My family could lend a hand but that would not be enough people. I spent some time in prayer and God told me to ask others. Soon, there were foreigners who either lived in Spanish Wells part of the year or "snowbirds" who vacationed long term and wanted to help us teach.

We began shortly thereafter keeping the kids in their grades and with each one of the volunteers taking one or two classes to help after school twice a week. This tutoring program helped form better relationships with the children and we branched into helping the kids on the weekend too. One girl I had befriended was a fiery leader in ninth grade. Her name was Nadege and she helped me get the kids together for anything we organized.

"Nadege, don't forget to come this Saturday with all the girls so we can continue," I said.

"But Ms. Amy we don't have any way to get there. Can you come get us?"

Without any transportation I knew it would at least take an hour to arrive at our house by foot, so I immediately responded "Yes."

Saturdays were now consumed with picking up the Haitian kids by making several roundtrips to Apea. Once at our house my kids and I would help with school work and I would allow the older High School children to use our computers to complete coursework. We also mixed in swim lessons at the beach, plus feeding the children at our house. This made for a full Saturday schedule. Whatever the need was, we wanted to meet it. And as the friendships grew, we were also able to make teaching the Bible our focus. Sandwiched in between the morning tutoring and afternoon swim lessons, we used lunch time to read the Bible and discuss it. The practice was nothing formal, but the kids liked it and so did our family. God was showing us how to be available and how to use this opportunity to show His love to these "sojourners" in the land.

He also was stretching me in more ways than I could imagine. One pivotal moment for me came when I had around twenty some youth in my house doing homework and using our laptop computers. As noon approached, they all were looking to me for the usual lunch. As I opened my kitchen cabinet, I saw I had one box of macaroni and little else. I also knew we had only one hundred dollars in our bank account with no

88

income in sight. As I stared in the cabinet, I could hear the Holy Spirit saying, *Go ahead, feed them, Amy.*

I thought about my family and stared at these Haitian children and knew I had to trust God's voice. As I directed the older girls to start cooking the macaroni, I climbed in my golf cart and headed to the store to purchase hotdogs and buns to add to the meal. When I returned, relief washed over me as I knew I had done as the Spirit asked. Watching the kids eat and laugh, I knew God wanted to see if I would obey Him.

As I read the Bible story later on from Luke chapter 3, God clearly told me He was pleased with my response on this day and that faith and obedience go hand in hand. As I came to verse 11, I read, "Whoever has two tunics is to share with him who has none, and whoever has food is to do likewise." *Thank you, Jesus,* I said inwardly. For on this day, the Holy Spirit's promptings had borne Jesus' fruit. I saw how giving of myself and my resources would allow me a fulfilling joy I had never inwardly experienced. It was like a hidden secret that was only between me and God.

Throughout the day I continued to thank the Lord for allowing me the delight in honoring God's opportunity to feed the teens. The peace and contentment I experienced from this one split second decision would propel me to have a deeper abiding trust in Jesus and to know that He would provide for me and my family as well. Amazingly, as God grew my faith in Him, He also grew the Haitian community's faith in me, my family and His ministry. The nudging from the Holy Spirit taught me more than I ever could have imagined about the necessity of obedience and the blessing of God given opportunity. When I yielded to Him in faith, I experienced Jesus. I felt a joy that was indescribable and an inward elation that no amount of money, possessions, or success could ever match.

It was at moments like these I began to see a direct correlation between giving love and receiving it in return as Ephesians 3:17–19 summarizes, "...so that Christ may dwell in your hearts through faith-that you, being rooted and grounded in love, may have strength to comprehend with all the saints what is the breadth and length and height and depth, and to know the love of Christ that surpasses knowledge, that you may be filled with all the fullness of God." For the first time I was experiencing the blessing of His presence within me.

It was also only months later that I understood meeting the needs of those children also afforded my family and me the trust and relationship that led me to share Jesus in those Bible readings. As it says in Mark 4: 8, "And other seeds fell into good soil and produced grain, growing up and increasing and yielding thirtyfold and sixtyfold and a hundredfold." God had implanted seeds and was multiplying love in our hearts for the Haitian people.

What the scriptures taught had become an inward reality. Jesus could take the little he gifted us with and use it for furthering His kingdom. This kingdom he was birthing in my family and me transformed our hearts into loving these precious Haitians. These people were becoming our people, people who needed love just like I did. A people who needed to know Jesus just like I did. A people who needed to understand that I loved them because of Jesus and His love for me first and foremost.

As we shared life with our new friends we began to talk more and more about Jesus and all He was doing for us, too. Little did we know at the time, but a ministry was unfolding right before our eyes. With Jesus at the center we were thankful to be living out what John 1:3 says, "God created everything through him, and nothing was created except through him." Everything God was doing in our lives was new and unexpected; we just had to focus on the main thing– Jesus.

God also reminded me what I been taught in previous Texas Bible studies which was the acronym J-O-Y. Putting "J"esus first, "O"thers second and "Y"ou last resulted in the abundant "Joy" He speaks about in Psalm 16:11, "You make known to me the path of life; in your presence there is fullness of joy; at your right hand are pleasures forevermore."

This new life God was creating was giving us courage to continue more and more on His path for our life. Yet alone with God I pleaded with Him for a game plan that would give us security beyond our daily existence. I still did not understand that my identity was already assured by the only thing that could ever bring JOY, the presence of Jesus Christ himself. But attaining this knowledge would come through many trials and onward we went.

Chapter 11

Saying YES!
The Blessing of Obedience

*I will surely bless you, and I will surely multiply
your offspring as the stars of heaven and as the sand
that is on the seashore.*

Genesis 22:17

Brrring.... The sound of the telephone rang in the distance, disturbing me from my half-sleep. Suddenly the lights flipped on and I heard Michael fumbling for the phone.

"Yes, hello?" He listened intently to the speaker on the other end.

"Oh, um, well, yes, let me speak to my wife. Can I put you on hold for a moment, Officer?"

Officer? I wondered. Just who was Michael talking to?

"Who is it honey?" I whispered as I saw he was covering the phone mouthpiece.

"Well it is a Bahamian police officer asking if we would be willing to take in a Haitian girl who has gotten in a fight with her Father. She is at the clinic now being treated."

"What girl?"

"Evans' daughter, Suzelynda."

"That is his daughter? I had no idea."

The girl I met at that Thanksgiving supper back in 2010 had reappeared at school. I'd heard from her own father she was a "bad girl." That she was just "trouble." Evans was a student in our ESL class and had become a close friend to my husband. What Michael had not been told was the violent abuse he had inflicted on Suzelynda and how she had run away repeatedly, terrified of his attacks. I, on the other hand had my own class of ladies and had not been privy to these firsthand conversations. I was aghast at the conflict Michael told me ensued in their home.

We didn't piece together that Evans was the father to this girl until we received that early morning phone call in April of 2012.

"Of course, we'll take her in. Don't you agree?"

"Yes, absolutely," Michael replied.

I remember the fond impression Suzelynda had made on me that first Thanksgiving in the Bahamas. I had reached out to her upon her recent return to Spanish Wells but did not know much about her at this point. She was the girl with the beautiful smile, I thought.

Michael returned to his phone call.

"Officer Albury, sorry for the delay. Yes, my wife and I agree and will definitely take her in tonight."

He hung up and I scooted out of the bed as Michael began getting dressed. Quickly I grabbed my robe and tiptoed into Luke and James' room.

"Boys wake up. I need you to get up and come into our room to sleep on the mattress."

"But Mama, it's late. Why?"

"Come on now, James. I'll carry you. I have someone coming who needs to sleep in your bed tonight."

I lifted James and took Luke by the hand into our room and laid them on the futon mattress in front of our bed. It had become a permanent fixture in our room and I was grateful for the extra space.

Suzelynda reached our house shortly afterwards. As Michael greeted her and the officer at the front door, I quickly straightened the boy's sheets and picked up a few of the toys strewn across the floor. Going back to the front living room, I thanked the Officer and escorted Suzelynda to the boy's room while Michael spoke quietly with the Officer at the door.

I put my arm around Suzelynda's shoulder but felt her pull away.

"It is going to be okay, sweetheart, I promise."

The terrified look in her eyes summed up the pain she was feeling, and her body language clearly showed the mistrust she must be experiencing. I took a risk and turned to ask her if we could pray. As we sat down on the edge of the bed, she nodded her head 'yes.' Without a word I watched as she closed her eyes and put her hands together to pray with me. Obviously, she was used to praying, I thought to myself. This encouraged me, but I silently wondered if she would be willing to open up to our family and especially me.

93

After I finished praying, I showed her the clothes I had gotten from the girl's room for her to sleep in. I handed her a washcloth and towel in case she wanted to bathe before she went to sleep.

"Suzelynda, help yourself to anything. Are you hungry or thirsty?" I asked.

She hung her head down low and nodded *no*.

"Ok, well I am here if you need me, so please just come to my room. You saw my door, right?"

Now she nodded *yes*.

As I climbed back into bed with Michael, I was careful not to wake the boys who were cuddled up together on the small mattress like sardines.

"Michael," I whispered.

"Yes, Hon?"

"What are we going to do? I just showed Suzelynda to the bedroom and asked her questions, but she did not even speak. Only used her head to respond "yes" or "no." I mean, how can we help her best?"

I felt nervous. Clearly, we were in uncharted territory. I sat propped on up my pillows with my eyes wide open in the dark.

"Well, we will do what we are always to do: act like Jesus," Michael said.

I sat there motionless, knowing of course Michael was right. After what seemed like hours, I finally sought God on my knees at the foot of my bed.

"Please God, show us how to help this precious child of yours. I don't know what to do or what to say but You do. So please help me to help her."

Daylight came soon enough with a knock at our door. The Officer who had requested Suzelynda stay with us returned promptly the next morning. Suzelynda was still asleep along with the rest of the household. It was Saturday when we typically all slept in, and since we had been awakened so abruptly the night before, Michael and I also had slept in, missing our daily alarm clock of the rooster crowing.

I went to answer the front door.

"Thank you for taking her in," the officer said. "No one else would, and I did not know who to ask until one of the locals said I should call you."

"No problem," I responded, "but what happened?"

The Officer hesitated and said he could not tell me specific details, just that there was ongoing abuse and this time Suzelynda had responded with violence back at her Father. Both had ended up bloody and bruised. The Officer thanked Michael and I profusely for being a temporary place for Suzelynda to reside and promised it would only be for a short time.

"The next step, Mrs. Boykin, will be meeting with Social Services and the Police Chief to discuss what will happen to Suzelynda. We will call and set up a time to meet with her at your house if that is okay."

"Of course," I said. Afterwards I turned to Michael privately, "Wow, what exactly did we get ourselves into? I had no idea that it would be this serious, did you?"

"No, but God did, and He wants us to be available, so we will," he replied.

I was reminded of one of my favorite stories from scripture. "Oh Lord, thank you for reminding me of the Good Samaritan." I said quietly. As I opened my Bible to refresh my memory, I turned to Luke 10:30–33 and read, "Jesus replied, "A man was going down from Jerusalem to Jericho, and he fell among robbers, who stripped him and beat him and departed, leaving him half dead. Now by chance a priest was going down that road, and when he saw him, he passed by on the other side. So likewise a Levite, when he came to the place and saw him, passed by on the other side. But a Samaritan, as he journeyed, came to where he was, and when he saw him, he had compassion."

At that moment I got it. *Thank you, Jesus, for more God-given opportunities to show compassion to someone in need.* I realized this was a gift from Jesus just like that first time I had responded by giving all my food to the kids at the Saturday club. This would be another way to show His love. Although many people whom I would have naturally assumed would have helped this poor child did not, that fact did not matter; my family and I had been given the opportunity to take Suzelynda into our home.

I finished reading the Bible story and looked intently into the last statements Jesus made to His disciples. Verses 36 and 37 say, "Which of these three, do you think, proved to be a neighbor to the man who fell into the hands of the robbers? He said, "The one who showed him mercy. And Jesus said to him, "You, go and do likewise."

Michael had said it so well but now I got it. Thank you, Jesus, for this awesome occasion to show your love. Armed with this confidence I was ready to help Suzelynda in whatever way showed Jesus' mercy.

Days turned into a week and as the time flew by I tried to get to know her better. Every day she would dress for school and head out with our children. Although she was living with us she never uttered a word. At lunch and dinner, she would make her own plate of food and sit quietly. After school, she stayed close by my side washing dishes or hanging clothes on the clothes line. Other than that, she would retreat to the boys' bedroom which had now become hers. Our family hardly knew she was living with us. She was quiet as a church mouse; although we all tried to engage her in conversation, she basically kept to herself.

One day many weeks later as we were hanging laundry, I told her, "Suzelynda, I love you and you can always count on me if you want to talk to me." Tears welled up in her eyes, but she just kept on hanging the clothes one piece at a time. My heart ached for her and as I had said the only thing I knew to say; I continued to look at her. I had no idea what to do so I prayed inwardly, *Please Lord give me your words and help me help her. Help me be merciful and compassionate like you told me to do.* As the tears fell, I gently hugged her and said a short prayer out loud.

Life went on like this for some time until four months went by. Little by little, our family began to see the girl who I had met at the Thanksgiving church outreach two years before. A smile would creep over her face and she even laughed. Finally, on one July day at the beach I looked out onto the clear blue ocean and saw Suzelynda grinning ear to ear as my youngest James tried to tackle her in the water. She tried to get away and was screaming happily, "No, James, no!" Although her words spoke "no" her expression clearly said "yes" as she laughed and splashed him with water.

James responded by jumping on her back and grabbing her long weave as he tried to climb onto her shoulders. She was laughing because her braided hair, which had been stitched onto her head, was now dangling in James' hand. Finally, I was beginning to see a glimpse of this beautiful Haitian daughter of the King emerge.

I still did not know any details about Suzelynda's life or the events surrounding that first night she arrived at our house. But I did know what I saw. Coat hanger scars on her back summed up a painful life. A two-inch scar on her forehead spoke volumes about what she must have experienced. I loved this sweet girl no matter what rumors I had heard about her being the supposed "problem" and a "bad girl."

The months went by and the meeting with the Chief Officer and Social Services finally came. After quoting scripture about living in the wilderness and having to obey God no matter what occurred in her Father's home, the Chief Police Officer summed things up by telling Suzelynda she was a minor and under the law, she had to comply by living with her parents. Anger and frustration welled up within me; I wanted to protect Suze as one of my own.

"But Officer, can she not just live with us and visit them?"

"No," he responded.

At first her father had entreated the government to ship her back to Haiti. He had called on them to do so, saying all this abuse was her fault for being a disobedient child. This was not unusual for the Haitian culture which teaches the men are in charge and always right.

But that did not matter, the most important part was the story was one sided and we knew only Evans' side. It seemed because he was now humiliated within his own Haitian community he was trying to act like a good Father and take her back. In his eyes this showed he was right, and she was wrong.

* * * * * * *

Tearfully, Suzelynda packed up her bag. "Suze, I want you to come over every day after school and all weekend. You are welcome here as much as you want," I told her.

THE WAY

It was her sixteenth birthday on that blistering hot August day. As we helped her pack to move back to her parent's home, I was angry at God and demanded, *Why?* But there was no answer.

Driving the golf cart toward her parent's house I could not stop thinking about her future with us at our home, her home. When we arrived at her parent's house, I put on my best smile and said, "Suze, don't worry, I am only a phone call away and God is always with you."

We clung to one another and finally she broke away.

"Ok, Mom." Quickly I shot my head up off her shoulder. *'Mom.' Is that what she said?*

"Suze, you must go back, you know I don't want you to, but you have to."

"Yea, I know. I love you."

"Oh, Suze how I love you too and so, so much. But remember Jesus loves you the most."

I was overcome with emotion and tried my best to hide it as I fought back the tears welling up in my eyes.

No, God, this is just a place; this is not her "home," I softly spoke as she exited the golf cart. Painfully, I watched the door shut behind her as she went inside the house. *Someday Lord, please someday soon; bring her home with us,* I prayed.

Chapter 12

IT'S OFFICIAL
God's Unleashing His Glory

And he gave the apostles, the prophets, the evangelists, the shepherds and teachers, to equip the saints for the work of the ministry, for building up the body of Christ, until we all attain to the unity of faith and of the knowledge of the Son of God, to mature manhood, to the measure of the stature of the fullness of Christ...

Ephesians 4:11–13

"I am a promise, I am a possibility, I am a promise...promise, promise with a capital "P." I am a great, big bundle of potentiality...yeah, yeah, yeah..." The Haitian children's voices rang out in my living room. Our ministry was now official and expanding. What first began as teaching English to the Haitian adults grew into tutoring their children in ESL and at the after-school tutoring program. From the after-school program we began spending time in their community and started our Saturday "club" as we called it at our house. This new happening turned into a friendship with the local Haitian pastor and his church. Now we took it a step further to meet with him.

"Pastor Peterson, how can we help you?" we asked.

"What if we start a Youth Group at your church with the young people we work with now?" Michael suggested.

"Wonderful, yes!" he excitedly replied. "We can also use help with our church expansion and needs."

Our mission was growing with The Haitian Peoples Church in Apea. Thursday nights became our official Youth Group night and Saturday's club remained the same with older kids coming out for tutoring, Bible study and swim lessons. Now we were able to shift our focus to intentional discipleship with specific students like Pastor Peterson's own daughter LaToya. I would tutor and teach Bible any chance I got. With a full weekly calendar now implemented, the Holy Spirit spoke to Michael about His ultimate plan for us.

At the same time, our financial situation was tenuous to say the least. For months and months, Michael and I had been praying about going back to Texas to solicit support from our Austin home church. We knew we had an actual ministry now and felt confident in sharing this news. We wanted to seek the church's support as well as the support of friends. In two years', time God had done a miraculous work. Now He wanted us to testify to not only what He had created but also how He had healed our family and marriage. Christ alone had changed us to look more like Him.

We hoped to inspire others by encouraging them how to be "all in" for Jesus. Going home to Austin would be like the woman at the well in John chapter 4 when she went back to evangelize her entire town. Verse 39 says, "Many of the Samaritans from that town believed in him (Jesus) because of the woman's testimony,..." After this woman had a personal encounter with Jesus, she was changed and went everywhere sharing the news of her transformation. I, too, was overwhelmed and wanted to share all Jesus had done for me and how He was changing me for His glory.

Spring Break would be the only time for our family to return to Texas since the kids had school off. The grandparents were desperate to see the grandkids and gladly offered to pay for our trip home. Interestingly, at this same time Michael met a mission team spending a day on the beach in Spanish Wells. The Leader of the trip, Mr. Clay, had given Michael his business card after Michael shared what our weekly routine was with the Haitian kids on the island. Mr. Clay urged Michael to consider hosting a mission team to come alongside us and help.

"I'm with the Fellowship of Christian Athletes," he said. "We're an organization that uses sports to communicate the gospel. It sounds like these Haitian kids don't have many opportunities to play sports. I could bring athletes down here to teach them anything they want and at the same time share about Jesus."

As Michael relayed the conversation to me, he said he thought it sounded like a good idea. Mr. Clay explained their teams would pay to come, covering costs for food and housing. It would be a win-win. We needed people to help us with the growing number of kids we served, and we needed financial support. Michael loved and played sports and I enjoyed them too. *Playing sports is an international language like the gospel is an international language* I thought.

For the moment though, we tabled that idea as we stayed busy with our new ministerial routine until our trip to Texas.

****

Very soon we were landing in Austin. Michael and I were excited to share our ministry news with everyone we knew. We had friends who offered to host a party for us where we could share God's unfolding plan for us in the Bahamas. We also had a meeting with our Texas church people, but as the week went on, I learned this trip was not going to turn out as I thought it would. Our friends warmly received us and were very excited to hear of God's work, but no financial support materialized.

Our home church also was excited and offered prayers, but no financial support came from them, either.

"Amy and Mike, we will definitely pray about it," Stewart the Mission Director said. "Let us know how it works out with other teams first and maybe we can send one later."

I was shattered. The reception at our church was lukewarm at best. This was the same church that was sending people all over the world on missions, the same church that had wanted us to go to Turkey, was excited about their own local mission yet uninterested about something God was creating right before their eyes. This was painful for me as both our friends and the church were willing to give us their time but not their hearts. Once again, I sought God with tears. I demanded, *Why God? Why?*

As we flew home with a heavy heart I prayed, *Are we not in Your will, Lord? Are we not doing the very thing you have asked us to do?*

Yet in my time of doubting God remained faithful. Weeks later during my morning prayer time I heard God clearly say, "Amy, if I would have allowed those people or the church to help you, I would not have received the glory, they would have."

Bewildered for a moment I pondered what God had said. Of course, He was right. I would have attributed any ministry success that would be forthcoming to the support of those people and their efforts and not God Himself. Clearly, my idol-worshipping heart was constantly in need of refinement.

I realized my stubbornness and determination to live by trusting in the people and systems I could see had once again failed. Connections such as friends and even our home church had failed us, but God would never fail us. I was learning to continually trust and allow the Holy Spirit to guide me instead of being led by my knowledge or rationale. I thought of the verse from Proverbs 16:1, "The plans of the heart belong to man, but the answer of the tongue is from the Lord."

Once again God was reminding me that just as I had to surrender to the initial call to come and follow Him, I must continually focus myself on Him and Him alone. My identity was not to be in anything, but Jesus and His guidance would yield His plan. Seeking to align myself continually with the Holy Spirit and learning to hear His voice was a lesson that had begun in this newness of living faith.

The miracle God had in store was right in the Bahamas and God had already prepared it ahead of time for us, we just simply had to continue to trust Him as it unfolded day by day. God answered my "why?" by having our local Bahamian church approach us asking if we wanted to work under their church doing the very ministry God had used us to birth. Being under their umbrella enabled our family to reside and work permanently in the Bahamas as an extension of the local church. Just as one door seemed to shut, God opened another one.

We were triumphant in the victory Jesus had already won! Now we would be a branch of the local body of Christ and be under the covering of God's church.

With incredible inward conviction and peace, Michael looked at me one morning a few weeks after our return from Texas and said, "The Holy Spirit is telling me I must call that FCA Trip Leader I met on the beach, Amy. Like right now."

"Ok, why?" I had already forgotten the beach encounter Michael had with the FCA Leader.

"Well…don't you remember the idea of bringing a team to help us? Now, is the time. That must be God's answer to provision and to the support and we need to step into it."

"Ok, Michael, make the call.

Quietly, I sat motionless on the sofa straining to hear the details of the phone conversation he was having until I finally heard him stop talking. Walking into the bedroom I asked somewhat anxiously,

"Well, what did he say, Michael?" I now had my hopes secured around this idea of a mission team.

"He said this call was clearly from the Lord. Only five minutes prior to me phoning him he was desperately searching for a place to bring a cheer team and baseball athletes on a mission trip."

"What do you mean?" I asked.

"Evidently, the team from North Carolina was supposed to travel to the Dominican Republic but the Coach felt it was too dangerous and asked to relocate to another country. When I told him you and I had been praying and thinking about hosting a team, he quickly interrupted me and asked if this August would be too soon."

Michael had a big grin on his face. I sat there somewhat stunned by what he had just said and thought to myself, *God you are teaching me a new way to hear you and obey.*

"Wow, that is so cool!"

"Oh, ye of little faith," he laughed.

Amazingly, this new relationship with FCA propelled us to formalize our ministry by getting a name. We had to have one to complete the approval process and become a partner with the FCA parachurch organization. We subsequently formed a non-profit to become an official religious organization. God knew exactly how to orchestrate all the details so that He would get us to this place. I was reminded of Proverbs 16:3, "Commit your work to the Lord, and your plans will be established." Our commitment required faith and once God saw our actions, He brought those plans into fruition.

We prayed a long time and asked God for the perfect name for this ministry. Finally, Michael and I had complete peace about naming it: *The Living Stone Ministry* sounded perfect. We based it on Scripture from I Peter 2:4–5 "As you come to him, the living Stone—rejected by humans but chosen by God and precious to him— you also, like living stones, are being built into a spiritual house to be a holy priesthood, offering spiritual sacrifices acceptable to God through Jesus Christ."

This passage is packed with a lot of truth, but we knew it summarized what we professed to believe about our journey as a Christ-follower. We knew as stones we must rely on Jesus, who is our chief Cornerstone but that we also need each other. We needed community to be a part of God's house, the church; to be able to live life with Jesus and show Christ-likeness to others.

A new chapter in our lives had begun. No longer would we be living by the daily manna God had provided for two years. Now, he was giving us fruit from the land. This fruit was both external and internal. Tangible income gave us a way to live and the ability to focus on the spiritual fruit birthed through evangelism and intentional discipleship.

That first mission trip came and sparked great interest in both us and the FCA Director to initiate more trips. One of the catalysts to do so was seeing the poverty in the Haitian community. At our first Sports Camp we saw children who did not have shoes or shorts. Most came that first blistering hot August day barefoot and in blue jeans to learn how to play baseball. We all were aghast. Even more concern arose when the FCA Leader found out these children did not know how to swim.

"How is it these kids can't swim when you live on an island surrounded by water?" He was shocked.

Teaching swimming lessons then became a necessary part of our mission trip activities. Although we had taught many of our Saturday Club Haitian children how to swim, there were many more children who needed instruction. Now, with the mission team enlisted as additional eyes, hands and feet on the ground we could teach others. We were even able to include Haitian children from another neighborhood in our sports mission week.

Thus, God grew His mission field and allowed us to serve over one hundred kids of all ages in that first camp. Using sports gave us a great avenue to communicate the gospel throughout each day of mission. In the morning we held a gymnastics, cheer and baseball camp then we would break for lunch where a mission participant would share about his or her relationship with Jesus.

In the afternoon we would swim and conclude with scripture and a short sermon. The week was a huge success as new friendships were formed and current ones strengthened.

It was funny when I thought about it—my family and I had never participated in a mission trip. This reality gave us a different perspective on what a mission trip should look like when teams came and served with our ministry. First and foremost, Michael and I wanted the time together to be about relationship. We had learned this was crucial to earning trust and we encouraged those coming to serve with us to forge friendships and spend time with the Haitian community. It was less about work or what we were doing, especially since we really did not have any typical mission trip building projects to do.

We had, instead, kids and parents in need of learning what it looks like to believe in Jesus and live like him. We would explain to the mission teams that the true servant, Jesus, says about himself in Mark 10:45 that he "...did not come to be served, but to serve,..." Serving people by loving them and equipping them with the Bible summarized the mandate Jesus gave in Matthew 22:37–40, "And he said to him, "You shall love the Lord your God with all your heart and with all your soul and with all your mind. This is the great and first commandment. And the second is like it: You shall love your neighbor as yourself. On these two commandments depend all the Law and the Prophets."

This was the standard by which we aspired to live, and we wanted mission participants to do the same: serve and love. After that first team left, we began receiving many more calls from various FCA groups to come alongside us the following year. Word obviously spread quickly throughout their network. These additional people were much needed and gave us the capability to better reach the Haitians by continuing to build relationships with them. In addition, at the end of that summer, the Haitian church whose members were being taught English decided to expand their own church. We came alongside Pastor Peterson to help with this project. By fall when it was complete, we were able to bring other mission teams to the church building to have Youth group with us as well as to the Sunday church service. This Haitian Community was indeed our family now and we were grateful for God's abounding opportunities.

As our ministry continued to grow by meeting more needs within the Haitian Community, our family flourished. Our children loved the local school and were doing well. They had formed many wonderful friend-ships with the Haitian and Bahamian kids and were serving and loving the Haitian community right along with us. The prayer God had planted in my heart to be a family-unified and serving Him-was coming into fruition! Indeed, the blessings were coming down as the prayers had gone up from our household throughout the past two years.

The one sad reality was our precious Suzelynda. After she returned to her biological parent's home, she became a less regular visitor at ours.

Initially, she would come to the house regularly, but as Fall went by, we saw less and less of her until it was hard to even find her.

I questioned her one day shortly after New Year's Eve in 2013 when she stopped by to spend the day with me. Cleaning the house together it felt like she had never left our home. As I was mopping, I asked her "Suze, how is home life?"

"Fine," she responded.

"You seem very happy and are smiling a lot, so things must be better right?" I asked.

But her response shocked me as she said, "No they just ignore me and act like I am not there, but that is ok because he does not hit me."

As tears welled up in my eyes, I turned away, but I asked if that is why I had heard she was not at home very much anymore.

"Yes, ma'am" she said. "When my Pa gets violent with me, I escape through my window, so I don't get beat."

"Where do you go?" I asked.

"I go hide in the bush," she replied.

I implored her to return to our home and stay with us as much as she wanted and thankfully, she began to do so. Now, since her father had no desire for her to be at his home and since the Police had fulfilled their duty within the law, we realized she could stay at our house if Suzelynda and her Father did not draw attention to themselves through violence. It appeared the police did not really care where she lived as long as her biological family life remained peaceful. That day I went to her home for the second time to pick her up I thanked God for answering the prayer I had uttered only a few short months ago.

"Suze, you are coming home!" I said joyfully.

With Suze back in place with us we were excited about the start to our new life. After two and a half years of remolding us and renewing our minds in Scripture God was about to unleash more of His majesty! We were now beginning to understand that we knew God in His fullness when we lived by abiding with Him through loving others. He had shown us through our faith journey that embracing His identity as our own yielded a new life that was changing our family from the inside out. Inward changes now manifested themselves with outward blessings. Armed with inward peace we knew we were living by Jesus and He was providing for us spiritually and financially. His grace really was enough.

SECTION THREE

FRUIT

*You did not choose me, but I chose you,
and appointed you that you would go and bear fruit,
and that your fruit would remain, so that whatever you
might ask the Father in My name, He will give it to you.
This I command you, so that you will love one another.*

John 15:16–17

Chapter 13

Unexpected Gifts

Thanks be to God for his indescribable gift!

2 Corinthians 9:15

"Michael, now that Suze is home, we need another bed. How will we get one from the US here?"

Looking up from his laptop he interrupted me, "Did you see this message from Ann, Amy?"

"No, what is it?" I said as he handed me the laptop.

The e-mail was short and simple. "Ms. Amy, hi! This is Ann from North Carolina. I just came on mission a few months ago leading the Cheer team. I have an idea and need to talk to you. Can we set up a time to talk on the phone? It is urgent so please let me know if you have time and I will be available. Love, Ann."

I really didn't know what to say. "Um what do you think, hon?" I asked.

"About the e-mail, I have no idea, but I would respond soon. It's sounds urgent. But if you are asking about the beds, I think you should ask around to the locals and see if anyone has a twin bunkbed they would be willing to sell us. That futon mattress on the floor is not comfortable for Suze and we need something else for her to sleep on. Hopefully we can buy one here instead of getting one from the US. Plus, honestly Amy, we need to be very careful with our finances. A few FCA teams have given us their deposits for the upcoming Spring mission trips, but other than that we don't have a lot of money to live on right now."

"Well, some money is better than none, right, hon? I understand it's all God's anyway and I am beyond grateful to have any income at all now. It is still quite amazing!"

As I pondered both the bed situation and the e-mail I turned to Michael. "Ok, let's pray. God will tell us what to do about Ann and the bed."

I realized that in a very short amount of time God had given me a kingdom perspective and was changing my mind to understand He was the Provider of everything. Instead of using my own logic and rationale, I was learning to seek Him in every detail. Doing so gave God the opportunity to show His Godness-His Greatness-His Glory. Now instead of worrying over how to pay for anything, I knew if it was His plan to accomplish His will He would provide. Jesus' words in Matthew 19:26 had become a reality, "With man this is impossible, but with God all things are possible."

For years I had prayed using Ephesians 3:20 as a model saying, "Please Lord do immeasurably more than I could think or ask according to the power you have given within me, so that Your glory will be revealed." Now, God was answering all my collective prayers that had begun at the onset of His call back in 2006. The unimaginable, the inconceivable, the unbelievable was becoming a reality.

If providing for us financially was not enough of a miracle in and of itself, establishing our family in a foreign country by providing a ministry and residency topped it all off. None of these things I would have prayed for or would have dreamt up. But living by faith was revealing to me a much bigger picture of what it really looked like and felt like to be a follower of Jesus. Experiencing God's truth proved to me the realities of Scripture. Now stories in the Bible such as Jonah and the whale were believable. Even Shadrach, Meshach and Abednego enduring the fiery furnace seemed plausible.

The next day, more surprises came.

"Guess what, hon?" Michael teased.

Before I could respond he continued.

"Mr. Clay just called, and not only does he have three more teams for us next Spring, but He asked if His Regional boss for FCA could come bring his family to serve with us after Christmas."

"Wow, really, that is so great! What does that mean?"

"I don't know but He is the Vice President of the Southeast division of FCA and that will be exciting to have someone of prominence from FCA come be a part of what God is doing here."

"That's awesome, but I still need to get back to call Ann," I responded.

I made the call and we connected.

After a lengthy conversation with Ann, I got a better picture of what was on her heart. She explained how she had never felt something so powerful before in her life as she had while serving with us in August. She went on to say she felt God was speaking to her to do more for the Haitian children. She had even been praying and had the idea to initiate a sponsorship for them to receive Christmas presents. Surprised by the idea, I responded by telling her I would pray and talk to Michael about it and get back to her.

"Michael, what do you think? Ann offered to set up a sponsorship program for the Haitian youth for Christmas gifts."

"Really?" he said.

"Yes" I responded. "She was so moved by the Holy Spirit this summer and feels led to do more. Isn't that amazing?"

"And she kept asking me about Teneesha, too."

"What do you mean?" Michael said.

"Well, I think she really has fallen in love with her. She asked about adopting her."

"Um, I don't know how that would happen Teneesha has a Mother; even though it seems like she would gladly give her away." The sad tone in Michael's voice showed me just how concerned he was.

Inwardly, I thought about it. *Surely, she would want to keep her precious five-year-old daughter, right?* But the Mother, Nikita, was tough and brash which made me think otherwise. She repeatedly had told me I could take Teneesha home with me any time I chose. I knew she was a prostitute who dated the local drug dealer. This Haitian girl was in my youngest son's class at school, so I thought I should ask him about her.

"James, what is Teneesha like at school?"

"She steals my pencils all the time and drives me crazy. She never sits down and is always roaming around the room. Mrs. Roberts gets really mad at her and usually sends her to the Principal."

"Oh, well how do you treat her James? You know it would be nice to show her Jesus by loving her and being kind to her."

Rolling his eyes, he said, "Oh Mom why do you always preach to us about Jesus?"

"Because He is the only reason we exist and everything we do should show who He is in us, James."

Please Lord, let my kids eventually understand that our life is "but a vapor" here on earth and we need to use every opportunity to be a light and show people Jesus.

Even if my own children grew tiresome of me constantly teaching about Jesus, I knew something must be working because the Lord was opening Ann's heart to these people just like He had mine. She saw a need and wanted to meet it. God was granting her faith and giving us Ann as an extension of a greater work He was doing in His ministry. As I pondered the opportunity more, I knew God was bringing Ann to us to grow our combined faith and evangelize the Haitian community. *Thank you, Jesus! Thank you, Holy Spirit, for this knowledge from you!* I whispered, praising Him.

Thrilled by her initiative, I emailed Ann and discussed the logistics of just how we might make this Christmas gift sponsorship work.

"What are ya'll thinking then?" Michael asked.

"Well, Ann is praying about setting up a sign at the front desk of the Gym where she works and asking people to sponsor a child for a Christmas present. She wants me to get a list of names and ages of the children together for her. If it works out, she will bring down the gifts and a team to do a Christmas give-away for the Haitian kids!"

From that first 2012 mission trip, God was growing Ann in her spiritual walk by being obedient and faithful to the desires He was placing on her heart. She had seen the need and wanted to meet it through her job and affluence. Not only was she a coach at the gym but her family owned the facility and she managed it as well. She had personal relationships that had been formed over many years and now she was ready to ask those acquaintances if they wanted to be a part of building God's kingdom with her and us.

It was a stretch of faith for both me and Ann as she first told me this idea. But, once again, God was far bigger. As Michael and I responded to Ann with an emphatic "Yes" on the plan, she and I both began to pray that people would respond with donations.

Ann was not a new Christian, but she was growing by actively living out her faith. "Follow me,..." is what Jesus commands of every believer as he told His own disciples in Matthew 4:19. It was evident Ann was responding to Christ's leading and had stepped out to accept this new challenge He had issued.

* * * * * * *

The Christmas gift sponsorship would require that I organize our ministry to make Ann's idea happen. As I gathered the Haitian children together again from both the Apea and Blackwood communities I got all their information. Since that first mission trip in August had included children of all ages from the two Haitian areas where they lived, Apea and Blackwood, it seemed only fitting that we include them both in the Christmas evangelism. My plan was to share the list with Ann so we could have individuals sign up for every child. "Michael, we have over one hundred and fifty children of all ages coming out now regularly!" I said excitedly. I could hardly believe it; I knew we were serving a lot of kids, but it was hard to tell since I never had actually counted them. God was doing this amazing thing right before our eyes and we were the recipients of this beautiful ministry He was growing. Writing this information down made it concrete and gave me more determination to use every avenue He presented to share about Jesus.

Finally, the weekend for Ann's visit arrived, and I raced in the taxi to pick her up. When she walked through customs with her friends, we immediately embraced one another like we had known each other for years, not months. Our ongoing e-mails and phone calls had definitely formed a lasting bond.

I squeezed her in a bear hug and jumped up and down. "Tell me who everyone is!" I finally said as I saw a circle of women standing by watching us.

"Oh, I am so sorry," Ann responded. "It's just that I'm excited to finally be here! This is my Mother-in-law, Sara Beth, and these beautiful women are my girlfriends. Sallie, Nancy, and Jennifer," Ann said with a beautiful big smile on her face.

After I welcomed everyone, I helped them with the many suitcases and got us all over to the taxi van. Pulling out of the airport, I could tell Ann was raring to go as she immediately asked, "Ok now Amy, what's the plan for the weekend?"

"Well, we have a lot to do in a very short amount of time. I was thinking tonight we spend all night wrapping the electronic tablets and get ready for the services that will happen tomorrow where we will hand out the Christmas presents."

"Oh, I am so glad you were able to ship in those tablets from US, Amy. That was a huge blessing because I don't think we could have lugged anymore suitcases. We each already have two!" Ann said relieved. "I was so glad I didn't have any issues getting the tablets or bicycles cleared through customs, but God showed us His favor. The Officers were really easy to work with when they arrived. I even have some locals helping us store the bicycles right now and they are going to help transport them and deliver them! The whole process was an answered prayer."

"What about having the Haitian girls over to make and decorate Christmas cookies? And can I go pick up Teneesha myself when we arrive in Spanish Wells, is that ok?" she asked.

"To your other questions, yes, to both. We can have all the girls over tomorrow morning early because we need to get the bikes and load them into our friend's truck to take them to the dock. You know we are doing two services- one in the Apea Haitian Community and the other in the Blackwood Haitian Community."

With our game plan determined our newly formed team of six (including me) got on task.

Ann's friend Sallie wanted to know what the plan was, too.

"Who gets what?" she asked.

"The younger elementary children are receiving bicycles and the older kids are receiving electronic tablets with extra memory cards. Ann and I prayed about it and we felt God telling us to do something they could use for school and recreation. And of course, something special that they could not afford for themselves." I replied.

"Oh, and I brought backpacks, hoodies, shorts and t-shirts for everyone too," Ann chimed in.

"Don't forget Ann, we also brought lots of hair ties and bows for the girls" said Nancy.

"Oh Ms. Amy, you won't believe what else we did. We got girls of every age from the gym to make hand-made cards with notes and even photographs of themselves for each child receiving a gift," Jennifer interrupted.

"You were able to do all of that for one hundred and sixty-four children?" I stuttered.

"Yes!" they all said together.

"Amy, we have other things too. I brought a sewing machine. I thought you or I could teach them how to sew. I have a lot of printables I brought too of scarves and I even have fabric and trims. I hope we will have time to try it out. But if not, it's all yours!" said Sallie.

"Wow, I am overwhelmed by you all. This is so amazing!" I said, choking back tears of joy.

Ann was beaming ear to ear. I could tell how proud she was to accomplish this huge project.

"And Amy, I want to go to the grocery store right away and buy the ingredients to make cookies, so we can start making them when we arrive. They need to be cool when the girls come to ice them tomorrow. Oh, and I brought a beautiful Bible to read the Christmas story from. Afterwards I want to break out one on one and share the gospel. Is that ok?"

"I can't wait to meet all of these precious children Ann has been speaking about, Amy. I feel like I already know some of them, even by name!" said Sara Beth.

The girls' team would only be with us for a quick four-day trip and we knew every minute was needed to accomplish our tasks. We began and ended our time together on the same high note, filled with the powerful presence of the Holy Spirit. In the end, the Christmas give-away was a success. We had gifts donated and many elated children and young adults.

But the greatest gift of all was the two church services we held where we preached the birth of Jesus. God allowed all of us the honor of bestowing tangible gifts only to share the only most meaningful gift we would ever need-His Son-Jesus. The entire experience strengthened my faith, Ann's faith, her friends' faith and my family's faith. Consequently, we all grew in trusting God exponentially.

As Ann and the team returned home from the whirlwind weekend Michael and I were blown away by God's faithfulness and privately prayed thanking Him. God was showing us the reality of 1 Corinthians 2:9, "What no eye has seen, nor ear heard, nor the heart of man imagined, what God has prepared for those who love him–..." God had allowed all of us to discern His way of divine love through the abiding presence of the Holy Spirit. His wisdom and ways transcended our earth-bound logic and showed us His plan from the sponsorship, to all the details of planning that finally culminated in the Christmas gifts was in actuality His way of revealing Himself to us. As we trusted the Holy Spirit in this faithful pursuit Jesus' presence was manifested in us and through us and we experienced His unexplainable joy.

The only cloud hanging over their visit was Ann's unrealized desire to adopt Teneesha. This precious girl was obviously abused even though there were no physical marks on her. Throughout the weekend Teneesha had stayed by Ann's side and had cried and screamed anytime Ann dropped her back at home. Ann even had nail marks on her arm showing how tightly Teneesha had clung to her. Clearly, this was not normal behavior from a child.

After the second day on the trip, Ann had pulled me aside and asked in a serious tone, "Amy, are you sure there is no way I can adopt her?"

"Well, although Nikita said yes she would allow you to take Teneesha to the US, according to international laws you can't. Teneesha does not have any legal status within the Bahamas or citizenship and is a minor who has a parent. Actually, she does not even have any identification."

"I am going home and seeking an international attorney. If the Lord has placed this on my heart, surely He can make it happen." Ann had tears streaming down her cheeks.

I hugged her and told her how grateful I was for her and we ended our time together praying, "Lord, we are overcome by You and You alone; for Jesus and the Holy Spirit and the ability to unite us by the gospel. We ask for you to will and work according to your plan for Teneesha and Ann. If you want Ann to adopt Teneesha allow this to occur and direct our steps in this endeavor. We ask this in your name Jesus. Amen."

"Amen," Ann whispered as the tears continued to stream down her face. We could do the only thing we knew, which was to turn the situation over to Immanuel-God with us-and hope that our desire aligned with His will.

As Ann and her friends departed, I made it a top priority to pray for this adoption as I continued to pour life into these Haitian pilgrims. Even though Ann's prayer for adoption did not materialize, eventually Teneesha was relocated to a home in another city where she was under the supervision of a Pastor and his family.

Other gifts came in unexpected ways but the greatest gift of all was the continual discovery of Jesus. As Ann and her friends had befriended our family, we saw the greater impact we were able to have together as we learned to revel in God's glory. Learning who He was in us, proclaiming His grace and watching lives become impacted by the gospel was the best gift we could ever experience. We were grateful God taught us that Christmas is truly about Christ being the one and only gift we would ever need or desire. It was our family's best holiday ever.

Chapter 14

Opportunities, Not Problems

*Then Caleb quieted the people before Moses, and said,
"Let us go up at once and take possession, for we are well able to
overcome it." But the men who had gone up with him said, "We
are not able to go up against the people, for they are stronger
than we." And they gave the children of Israel a bad report of the
land which they had spied out, saying, "The land through which
we have gone as spies is a land that devours its inhabitants,
and all the people whom we saw in it are men of great stature."*

Numbers 13:30–33

"Merci, merci."

People crowded around as Michael and I walked up to the door of the Apea Haitian Baptist Church. The women swarmed us, hugging tightly as the men patted Michael on the back. Heads were nodding, and everyone had big smiles on their faces.

"You are so welcome. All of you are so very welcome but remember all of the gifts were just because we have the most important gift bestowed upon us-Jesus," I reminded them.

Ah, oui, Merci Jezi!" Ms. Chedeline from my ESL class said.

We filed inside the church with our friends.

"Ok everyone let's open in prayer. Settle down now," Pastor Peterson implored the small group of Haitian couples.

Everyone huddled together, and Michael and I listened to their predicament.

As tourism was beginning to blossom near the Apea Haitian Community, many of the people were being told by the local Bahamians to vacate their land. The Bahamians had allowed Haitians to build little communities on their properties, charging a rental fee for electricity and use of the land but now economics dictated their future. One other nearby community had already been condemned. The tiny interwoven shacks of homes were bulldozed, leaving some of our families homeless and scrambling.

Because of our background in real estate, Michael and I understood this waterfront property was prime real estate and would no doubt be marketed for sale. Still, we weren't sure of the best way to help.

The only solution was for the Haitians to migrate to the mainland of Eleuthera to a larger Haitian settlement-Blackwood-which was located on this island a ten-minute boat ride away. Since we had included the children from this area in that first summer mission Camp in 2012 and presented them with gifts and a Christmas service the week before, we discerned God was on the move uniting these Haitian communities to-gether. The only issue was would the Apea community embrace going to the Blackwood community? Blackwood had a reputation of being a scary place. I had gathered details from my ESL students and heard that even people who live in Apea did not want to associate with the Haitians in Blackwood. Residents told me they were the poorest people and crime was a significant problem. We wondered how much poorer one could be since we knew the Haitians in Apea were also living in this condition.

But God always knows best; if it was His will for these communities to combine, He would indeed provide the way. That day what seemed like a problem to the Haitian people was God's gateway to another chapter of our lives. Although the couples were clearly distraught, God was teaching me that what we call "problems" are really His opportunities. I thought of Romans 8:28, "And we know that for those who love God all things work together for good, for those who are called according to his purpose." If God was God, I had to see this situation as He did-as opportunity and another new beginning.

A tentative game plan was made to investigate and see how we and other Americans could help finance homes for the Haitians. Hugging my precious ladies goodbye, I tried to reassure them with big smiles. Since they had learned some English in our classes now, I told them, "I love you all and would never let my family become stranded. Don't worry, we are all God's family too and He won't let you down, I promise."

Michael went full force into gear heading over to Blackwood to check out the area. When we had included the children from Blackwood in our first summer mission camp, we had found an older boy, Jean, and had him coordinate getting the kids over to our island via the ferry. We had also done one outreach with friends that same summer going to some of the houses on the main road in Blackwood. But really, we had never actually spent a considerable amount of time in the community itself.

Hesitantly, I asked Michael, "Are you sure you are ok to go over alone?"

"Of course! Are you going to listen to the rumors about Blackwood being a bad neighborhood? You, Amy, of all people!"

I felt like he was chastising me.

I stuttered back, "Well, I don't know, I hear there is prostitution, drugs and voodoo. Why don't we pray before you go?"

We bowed our heads together and Michael prepared to leave.

As I left Michael at the dock and watched him go on the short boat ride across the water, I prayed silently that God would place a hedge of protection around him. Thankfully, I did not have a lot of time to stew in my doubts since the after-school program was about to begin. Students were waiting when I arrived, and this caused me to stay later than usual before I headed home. When we pulled into the driveway of our house after dinnertime, the kids and I noticed Michael was not home.

"Where's Dad? Didn't you tell us he was coming home an hour ago?" Luke asked.

I began to worry because it was getting dark and Michael had not returned. I tried reaching him on his cell phone and just then he opened the front door. Relieved I gave him a hug, "So? How was it? Why were you gone so long?"

He replied in a way I had not seen in some time, radiating such enthusiasm and peace.

"You won't believe it, Amy. After I got off the boat, I saw Jean, the boy who helped us get the kids over every day for the Camp. He walked me up the trail everyone uses to get into Blackwood."

"Trail?" I asked.

"You know there are not many people with cars, they can't afford them, so most people walk. Anyway, after passing many goats and pigs we reached the road-you know that main road that goes down the center of Blackwood-and I just stood there for a while after Jean said he had to go home."

"I started walking up and down that road and it was amazing. One child would pop out of a house, then another, and another, and on and on. Finally, I had a group of kids of all ages surrounding me and giggling. Some I recognized from our Christmas service, but many were new."

"Wow, that is awesome. So, I take it there are a lot more people?" I asked.

"Oh yes. I was there so long because the kids and I started playing games on the soccer field. Just kicking their soccer ball around; the time went so fast! But, Amy, the poverty is worse. No one had shoes and most of their clothes were tattered."

"Well, we saw some of that in August."

"Yeah, we did. But I'll tell you, their joy, the smiles, their hearts were so full of love. I felt the Holy Spirit as soon as I saw those children. This is why God brought us here."

"What?" I said somewhat stunned.

"I know God wants us to help this community. This is the ultimate plan."

Michael sat down and untied his shoes. "And this is where we need to bring our friends next week after Christmas."

"You mean the Harris Family? The FCA Regional Director?" I asked.

"Yes, this is where we will have camp every day."

"Where, in Blackwood?" I was shocked.

"On that big open grassy place, they call their soccer field or, excuse me, 'football field.'"

* * * * * * *

The day of that conversation was pivotal for our family as Michael had heard the Holy Spirit beckoning us to grow our ministry. When our new friends, the Harrises, arrived from Georgia, we did indeed take them every day to Blackwood where we held the same sort of sports camp, we had previously in the summer months.

One day as Mr. Harris was walking through the community, he noticed something Michael had already homed in on-plastic milk crates affixed to the top of light poles being used as basketball hoops. Mr. Harris was a former College Football Coach and we had used his American football expertise at the camps. Now on the last day of his family's trip he pronounced to Michael and me, "We are going to build you a basketball court!"

"A basketball court?" we excitedly asked.

"Yes, kids need a place to hang out. Although the field is somewhat cleared away for soccer, a court could be built there, and it will anchor the Community. But most of all it will be a great place to evangelize," he said.

We watched him eye the electrical post where the milk crates were affixed, and he pronounced, "Build a court and they will come."

Thus, our ministry grew and shifted to the Blackwood neighborhood full time. With some of our Apea families coming over to Blackwood we now began another chapter of meeting new children and families.

Michael and I again privately thanked God for the possibility, for sending a man who saw a tool that could be used for ministry and the desire to fulfill it. We prayed it would indeed happen-the building of the basketball court-but quite honestly, I was skeptical. *Why would Mr. Harris make such a large donation to build a court for free and not want something in return?* I wondered.

God, in His way, was teaching us that He alone was in control and that His thoughts were the opposite of the world's thinking. Scripture such as Luke 6:38, "...give, and it shall be given unto you. Good measure, pressed down, and shaken together, and running over, will be put into your lap. For with the measure you use it will be measured back to you," had meaning if we followed Christ.

In direct contrast we had been raised with the mindset to hold onto to as much as we could. Even the 10% tithe to our church had been difficult to give away. We had also been taught a worldly system of amassing wealth as security. This stronghold was being shattered by Mr. Harris' generosity. We could now see how our mindset was in direct contrast to God's. Whereas I had placed hope in my "contacts" and "connections" back home to give and support us, God showed me repeatedly He was quite capable of bringing whomever He chose to build His kingdom. He was God after all and He was making sure I understood He could do anything. Looking at scripture I began to understand that God's character did not change.

Hebrews 13:8 says, "Jesus Christ is the same yesterday and today and forever." If God says He is unchanging then that meant He did not see our challenges as problems.

God had already proved He would allow situations just like everything we had experienced to get to this point in order to show how big He is. When I thought a situation like moving Haitians to another community looked difficult, I was learning to change my mind to see God's favor instead. If I doubted funds would be sent for a basketball court, then how could I really believe God is who He said He is? As I began studying more intently God's nature, I found Exodus 34:6 where He said about Himself, "I am the LORD God. I am merciful and very patient with my people. I show great love and, and, and I can be trusted.." This was my God. I was growing and learning to change my thinking to align with His.

* * * * * * *

The post-Christmas visit with the Harris family came to an end and we hugged our new friend's goodbye with grateful hearts. We were immensely thankful for the Christ-centered fellowship and friendship we had developed while they were with us. However, I was still uncertain if Mr. Harris would really carry through with a donation to build the basketball court he envisioned in the Haitian community.

Although the US was still rebounding from the economic recession this was even a better reason for God to show up and prove He alone could provide financially for a basketball court. At the beginning of the New Year, we promptly heard from Mr. Harris. He let us know he was sending us the full amount of money as promised. God was growing my faith-faith to believe and trust in Him alone to accomplish his task-faith to believe that He could move hearts to further His kingdom and faith to understand that money was just a tool to glorify Him. I was learning my family and I were vessels and that God was allowing us to participate in this wonderful opportunity. God was using us and others to make His name known in this new Haitian community we were now focusing our lives in.

It took six weeks to line up the construction schedule and order the necessary materials but given that this was occurring in a foreign country, we were excited to begin building by the middle of February of 2013. One Saturday we arrived on our Blackwood field to see many women and men lined up across the property.

"What's going on? It's only 7:30 in the morning," I asked.

There were ladies dressed in brightly colored yellow shirts spread out all over the field gathering stones and putting them in piles. None of them knew English so they all smiled when I asked my question. Luckily, Pastor Phillipe, a local Haitian man living in the Blackwood community, came down the road waving and said, "Good morning my Brothers and Sisters in Christ! These are my people coming to help with the stones!"

We had met Pastor Phillipe on several occasions and respected his authority and leadership within the Blackwood community. He preached as an Associate Pastor at a church forty-five minutes away and worked at a hotel in a nearby town.

"So, Pastor Phillipe, the ladies are here to help?" I replied.

"Yes, of course, they already have been cleaning and getting rocks for the basketball court."

"Why do they all have the same shirts on?" I asked.

"To make sure you know they are the ones here to help you!"

Wow! I thought. *God brought a man from Georgia to a family from Texas living in the Bahamas to help a people from Haiti. What an amazing picture of the nations and what an amazing picture of the gospel at work.* I was thankful God knew how to make scripture like 1 Corinthians 12:14 a reality, "For the body does not consist of one member but many." I knew God was growing us all and we needed one another so His kingdom in Blackwood could be built. The rocks were the foundation for not only a basketball court but for a community to worship Jesus Christ.

I reflected on the thought that we were different rocks like the different parts of the body of Christ as 1 Corinthians 12:18–20 reads, "But as it is, God arranged the members in the body, each one of them, as he chose. If all were a single member, where would the body be? As it is, there are many parts, yet one body."

We may have physical distinctions and originate from different cities or for that matter different nationalities but collectively our belief in Jesus merged us as the universal body of Christ. Joined in Christ, we felt God's amazing presence of the Holy Spirit.

"Thank you, Jesus! Thank you, Jesus," I said repeatedly out loud as we put hundreds of rocks down for the court. Laughing to myself I thought, *thank you for a Pastor who understands the importance of being a united team.*

It may have been small to others, but the yellow shirts signified our commonality and I loved Pastor Phillipe's discernment and vision. This court became the foundation to proclaim and further God's kingdom in Blackwood. Now, with adults and children seeing our family's passion for their people, more people entrusted us with their lives and we thanked God that new friendships began unfolding.

Chapter 15

Unity – One in the Spirit

...that they may all be one, just as you, Father, are in me, and I in you, Father, that they also may be in us, so that the world may believe that you have sent me. The glory that you have given me I have given to them, that they may be one even as we are one, I in them and you in me, that they may become perfectly one, so that the world may know that you sent me and loved them even as you loved me.

John 17:21–23

Working side by side on the basketball court for many weeks gave our family rich friendships and great peace. It reminded me of the early church in Corinth Paul described in 1 Corinthians 10:3–4, "...and all ate the same spiritual food, and all drank the same spiritual drink. For they drank from the spiritual Rock that followed them, and the Rock was Christ."

The building process also afforded us time to get to know the adults whereas in the past we had gotten to know only the teens and children. More importantly, it allowed us to be present as disciple-makers in the community. In Mark 3:14 it says, "And He (Jesus) appointed the twelve, so that they would be with him." We were now "with him" Jesus, and to be able to make more disciples we were now also "with" the Haitian community at large. This relationship grew into a trusting bond which allowed us to become unified. The community surprisingly rallied around the project and made it their own. We in turn were blessed with learning more about the people with whom we worked. As our hearts were opened to the various plights they faced, God showed us the needs in different families such as food, clothing and medicine. Since we spent every day in Blackwood, the Haitians felt free to come communicate what they needed.

As I was sitting in the Pavilion one day, teaching a Bible story to the younger Haitian children, one of the girls said to me, "Ms. Amy, I heard Samuel was stealing food."

"He is going over to other people's house and going in and taking the bread off the table," Anaica went onto say.

Samuel was a precious three old boy, the youngest of nine children all raised without a father. His Mom worked but food was still scarce. Making only approximately fifty U.S. dollars a week proved insufficient for survival. After speaking to Samuel's mother Gina about how we could help her provide more food for her family, we came up with a plan to supplement their income by purchasing more groceries. Eventually, we had her older son Peterson come live with us for a year, to disciple him and provide him a better education at our local school, lessening the financial load for Gina.

Another opportunity to show God's love arose one day when two twin boys, Joseph and Junior, approached me with their mother. "Ms. Amy my Pa don't have no work now and we don't have no food," Joseph said.

"Boys, tell your Mom that I will pick her up every Monday and take her to the shop and she can get food for the week. Does that sound ok? Tell her I will pay for it."

Joseph interpreted for her; she smiled and nodded *yes.*

Ms. Marie from my ESL class was yet another woman we discovered with a desperate need. She had diabetes that was taking a tremendous toll on her body.

"Amy, she could die. You must get her help and immediately," said Renee. Renee was Mr. Harris' daughter and had come on a medical mission team to serve the ministry.

Soon stories like this began unfolding and each time we did whatever we could to meet the need. Healing was being poured out not only on the Haitian people but also on our own family. Just as it says in Psalm 147:3: "He (God) heals the brokenhearted and binds up their wounds," spiritually and physically God was healing and nourishing us. As we poured out love to these people by meeting their needs, we felt Jesus' love fill us up and amazingly our wounds of the past were healed as well. Our desires to seek the things of the world and hold up things as idols to cure our emptiness were gone now. Instead, the dream God had given of living life as a family for His glory was being lived out every step of the way.

Joy abounded as our family worked alongside our Haitian brothers and sisters to complete the construction of the basketball court. With the completion of the basketball court in May, we were excited to continue the team momentum God had created during the building process.

One day Pastor Phillipe came to us with another question.

"Amy and Michael, our stage needs repairing; can you help with this now?"

We really liked Pastor Phillipe and were enjoying getting to know this man who aspired to shepherd the Blackwood Community. Immediately we responded *yes* but later thought to ourselves, *how much will it cost? And how will we pay for it?* But God already had the answer prepared as He sent provision from sponsorship solicited by the ministry. Many people were indeed willing to donate towards building God's kingdom in Blackwood!

THE WAY

What the Blackwood community had called a "stage" previously, we decided to enlarge and cover properly so it could function as a place where we could hold ministry activities. With the necessary money through donations from mission team participants we excitedly began construction.

One Saturday as my family and I were working on the construction of the new pavilion I spied an older boy on a bicycle. He had been coming around curiously checking us out as we were working. Day after day we returned and this young man, who looked to be in his early twenties, sat on his bike in the corner of the field. He acted like he could care less about our activity, but it was obvious from his stance he was clearly interested.

After three days I decided to walk over and introduce myself.

"Hi, I'm Amy. Who are you?"

"Davidson," is all he said, not smiling. His answer was curt, his voice full of pride. I tried to engage him in small talk but only learned he had attended school in Spanish Wells and had graduated a few years ago. The one thing I could tell was he was a leader. Boys would pass him and hail him as if he was the boss of Blackwood. *He will build Jesus' kingdom in Blackwood,* I thought to myself privately. The next day he and some of his friends hooked up speakers and music directly across from where we were building and began playing loud ugly music full of verbal slurs and expletives. *Obviously, Davidson is showing me who is the chief of this town,* I thought. I was up to the challenge.

While my family and I worked on the pavilion we listened to this offensive music blaring from the speakers until I could no longer stand it. I got down from my ladder and marched over to the teen boys and told them, "WE are here to honor Jesus! You can see that we have young children too. Why don't you turn that music down or off?"

Davidson and his crew glared at me. After all, this was their home-not mine. As we stood there in silence, I decided to take the opportunity to introduce myself to the other boys with him.

"Hi, I am Amy. We used to help the Apea Haitian Church but now since our friends have moved over here to Blackwood, we want to help ya'll too."

"Are ya the ones who built the court?" one of the boys asked.

"Yes. Well actually, no. I mean, God had an organization called FCA build the court for this community, so you can come play basketball," I responded.

At that point the atmosphere shifted. Davidson and his clan each shook my hand and told me their names. From then on, they were intrigued by us and started to come out and help with the construction. Eventually they would learn about Jesus too and by June of 2013 the Blackwood Haitian Community had been physically transformed. But the biggest transformations were yet to come.

When mission teams came, we would bring them to Blackwood and continue what we had already been doing since the beginning. Our family's weekly routine of Bible studies for various age groups, meeting the physical needs of the adults and teaching ESL set a great foundation, but once teams came alongside us, we could be more effective in reaching the community with the gospel. We realized the field was our church. God had miraculously created an area that was becoming our "ekklesia." In the original Greek *ekklesia* means 'called out ones.' I learned that it meant a place where people gathered or assembled.

God had created an area that had become our church, a place where we-His chosen people- could come together, teach the gospel and live it out. This made complete sense since the community did not have a church building and the closest one was twenty minutes away. Since cars were scarce in this poor area, transportation to get to church was an issue as well. God was gathering His people together using His resources and we simply were the chosen instrument to do His work.

We used the soccer field for the sports we were teaching, the pavilion was where we had Bible lessons and the basketball court was another area for games or gatherings. Evangelism was occurring, and heart transformations began when we welcomed our third mission team from St. Simons, Georgia. One leader, a Pastor, had a tremendous impact on the Blackwood teens. By the end of the trip, we had confessions of faith and held our first baptisms.

Two Haitian boys and one Haitian girl repented from their former lives and turned to Jesus as their Savior. One of them was Davidson. The other was Davidson's good friend Jean. Jean was the young man who had helped us at our first summer camp with our first mission team by organizing and leading the Blackwood kids daily to the camp. The girl, Nadia, was an older teen who also was a leader in the community. These three set the precedent for others. Now kids wanted to become like their brothers and sisters who were filled with a newness that was tangible. Soon more Haitian teens and older children would step forward seeking to know Jesus and decide to follow Him.

Life continued in our Blackwood church field with a weekly routine that began a new chapter of discipleship with these older Haitian leaders. To be a "disciple" of Jesus means to be a student or learner. The difference now for these teens was they understood that being a "Christian" was more than a title; it meant an entire life turning towards their Teacher, Jesus. The only way to do this was to learn the Bible and apply it to daily life. That is exactly what they began to do.

The power of the Holy Spirit had been ushered in with our arrival but now God unleashed His power and authority from that moment on with those who worked alongside us. By the end of the summer of 2013, many teens proclaimed Jesus Christ as their personal Savior and started the journey of following Him. With every mission team who worked with our family, we taught more and more about who Jesus was and why we should abide by Him. As this happened, God moved more teens to make a profession of faith. Now scripture like Acts 1:8 was being lived out, "But you will receive power when the Holy Spirit comes upon you. And you will be my witnesses, telling people about Me everywhere-in Jerusalem, throughout Judea, in Samaria, and to the ends of the earth.

As the seeds were being planted in the hearts of the Haitian kids, amazingly, they also were growing in the US team participants. Many young adults also either dedicated or re-dedicated their lives to Jesus and were baptized or came back on subsequent trips to be baptized! God's Way was indeed unfolding. My family and I shared life with these wonderful Haitian people and team members, but God alone unveiled His glory through the power of the Holy Spirit upon us all. He was working powerfully to change the hearts and minds of many.

The awesome things Jesus did in the Bible were a reality now and our family understood the power of the Holy Spirit and the correlation of being faithful to Him. John 14:12 came true, "I tell you the truth, anyone who believes in me will the same works I have done, and even greater works, because I am going to be with the Father." Jesus' obedience to the Father's gave mankind the opportunity to not only have a relationship with Him but also have the same or greater power by the indwelling of the Holy Spirit.

With summer coming to an end, Michael and I decided we wanted to celebrate all Jesus had done to bring us to this point on our journey. But that plan would have to be put on hold. The day after our last mission team left, we suddenly received a text at 4 am.

"What does it say Michael?" I grumbled. The repetitive beeps kept alerting us to messages coming through, disturbing my sleep.

"Oh no, Amy, wake up, wake up now!" There was alarm in Michael's voice.

As I sat up fumbling for the lamp switch, Michael announced, "There has been a raid in Blackwood, they have beaten and taken a lot of our people!"

The news startled me awake. I shot up in bed and because I didn't know what else to do, I did the best thing—knelt next to my bed to pray. Gripping my face in my hands I cried, *Lord what now? What can we do Lord but trust You? Oh, please help us to help your precious people!*

Chapter 16

Deliverance

Now the Lord is the Spirit, and where the Spirit of the Lord is, there is freedom.

2 Corinthians 3:17

We had heard about the raids on Haitian communities and knew they were a possibility, but the last one was over five years ago. Now the government had sent the Bahamian Defense Force, the equivalent of the US Navy, to surprise the Blackwood community.

"Michael, what exactly are they looking for?"

"Haitian people residing in the country illegally."

"So, they have to show they have residency, Michael?"

"Honestly, Amy, I don't know. I suppose since an election is coming, they're ramping up again. We will have to see what happens."

I was ill prepared for the trauma and emotion I was experiencing. After the early wakeup call that morning from our trusted friend Jean, Michael and I decided we had to immediately go over to Blackwood and check on our friends. Jean could not say much but told Michael in a low whisper he had run away from the Police and was hiding in the bush.

We waited for the first ferry to begin operating that morning. I sat at the dock anxious and scared, praying silently to myself. Finally, 7:00 am came and we hopped onboard, making it to Eleuthera in about ten minutes. *Soon we'll find out what's happened to our beloved sojourners,* I thought.

As we walked up the trail to Blackwood an eeriness crept around me. I don't know if it was because of the still Summer morning but it was as if the trees were anxiously watching and waiting for someone to appear. I penetrated the foreboding silence with a song to comfort myself. Thankfully God reminded me of one of the verses we had just taught the Haitian children the prior week. The chorus repeated Psalm 56:3, "When I am afraid, I will trust in You O Lord, when I am afraid, I will trust in You. Oh, oh, oh…"

The tune replayed in my mind and I comforted myself singing God's Word out loud. Whether I was warning the unforeseen enemy or harkening to angels, I didn't know but I started praying, *Oh Lord I hope the children remember this too and are saying your very words.*

As we arrived at the main street of the village there wasn't a soul in sight. The Bahamian Defense force was long gone by now, so I stood in the street holding onto hope that all were safe; I knew that was not the case. Jean had made it clear there had been violence the night before as he had been awakened to the sounds of men shouting and a door being busted open.

Walking by the houses, I saw curtains gradually pulled back from the windows and relief washed over me. *Signs of life! Thank you, Jesus.* Finally, sweet Esterline, a beautiful four-year-old girl, came running down the street.

"Ms. Amy, Ms. Amy!" she screamed. With her arms outstretched she jumped into my embrace and wrapped her tiny legs around me. We both began sobbing. She was gripping me so tightly I could hardly move so I decided to plop down right there in the middle of the street. As I cradled her back and forth, she said, "They took my Mommy, Ms. Amy, they took her."

Over and over she repeated the words and finally I composed myself enough to say, "Ok, Esterline, it is going to be okay sweetheart. Do you know where your Daddy is now?"

"I don't know," Esterline said as she choked on her tears.

"Don't worry sweetheart, God is with them both," I said, fighting back sobs doing my best to sound assuring. Clinging in my arms, she continued to cry loudly as I rocked her back and forth. Slowly other children began to creep from the bush and their homes and came cuddling around my legs. Esterline's two-year-old brother Emmanuel was one of them. Grasping my calves, he hugged me tightly.

As Michael approached me and the kids he asked, "Where are their parents?"

"They don't know. "Gone" is all Esterline says," I responded.

"Well, from what I have pieced together from those I can find, most of the adults are hiding in the bush but many were taken," Michael told me.

"Bush? You mean all the farmland surrounding this Blackwood Community? What about the children?" I asked.

"Yes, evidently some were taken too."

138

"Oh no!" I cried and let the tears roll down my cheeks as Esterline held tightly to me. "Do you know what happened?"

"The Bahamian National Defense Force came around four am when we got those text messages and started banging on doors, asking for identification and paper work to reside legally in the Bahamas. Some people ran and when they did, they were caught and taken. Others were taken forcefully from their houses. Either way, we need to go find where they are detaining our people and see if we can't get them out. I already called the car rental company to see if a car is available, but they aren't open yet, so I left a message. As soon as they call me, we can go and find where they are detaining everyone."

"I heard they probably are at the meat packing house, so we could stop there," Michael added.

As we waited for the rental company to open, we walked from house to house and took an account of who was missing so we knew who to look for later on. Most of the teens and adults were gone which left the young children at home without any supervision or care.

"Michael, we can't just leave the children here all alone. They are terrified," I said.

"Ok, why don't we call our ministry interns in Spanish Wells and have them come over now?" he replied.

"Do you think they are ready for this? I mean emotionally ready Michael?"

"I guess we will see," he replied.

Earlier on the FCA Spring mission trip, Mr. Clay had made the suggestion of having college students come as interns for the Summer to help us out. He saw we had a lot on our plate taking care of various teams as well as ministry and told us how FCA partners with other outreaches by bringing interns along to support the work. We were open to the idea after many precious students had asked us to consider them as interns after serving one week in the Spring.

We now had three girls who remained after a long Summer of many team visits and were grateful to be able to call them for help. Blakeley, Carly and Amber were amazing servants and I knew they would jump right in regardless of this circumstance. I just hoped they were emotionally ready.

As I called Blakely, I tried to compose myself, but she could tell from the sound of my voice the severity of the situation.

"Blakely, we need you three girls to hop on the ferry and come on over to Blackwood now. There has been a raid and the kids need us."

"What do you mean 'raid' Ms. Amy?" she asked.

"Well," I paused, "in the Bahamas the Bahamian Defense Force can come at any time and ask the Haitians for the proper paperwork to reside in the country. Some of them might have it but some do not. If they're here illegally, they can be deported back to Haiti."

"You mean they would send them back to Haiti?" Blakeley asked.

"Yes, it is the law and they can."

"What about the children?" she went on to ask.

"I don't know Blakely; we are still gathering information, but I can tell you they need us now and we need you and the girls to come on over and care for them."

While we waited for the interns to arrive Michael and I walked the streets and saw remnants of broken doors where the police had entered several houses. We began to speak to the few adults remaining in the community and learned that as some ran from the police they were badly beaten. Doors had been broken into to get to others that the Bahamian Defense Force believed were resisting arrest.

Painful tears streamed down my face as I suddenly felt the Haitian's plight firsthand. To be a refugee was hard enough in its own right. Living in a foreign country without any legal status was challenging but the system, although harsh, was legal. I knew their hope could only be found in the gospel.

Thank you, Jesus, this is why you sent me and my family here to the Bahamas. You sent us to these precious sojourners to share the only thing they need, which is You.

Michael interrupted my thoughts, "Come on Amy, we are going to take a taxi to go to the rental place; they just called me to say they are open."

"Ok let's get the girls situated first, hon."

As the girls arrived, I met them on the field and slowly the hugs and tears began to subside as they gathered all the kids and started playing games with them. Soon laughter and joy rose from the soccer field and once again I felt grateful to God for our small collective part in helping His people. As we told the girls our plan to go find those who were being held at the makeshift jail, I asked them and the children to circle 'round so we could pray.

"Father, God, you are our Abba, Daddy. You teach us in your Word that You, Jezi, are always with us in the storms of life. We speak to this storm just like you did in Mark 4:39 saying "Quiet! Be Still!" We also rejoice knowing You are our refuge and help in this time of trouble. What was meant for evil can be used for our good and most importantly for Your glory. So today, we say thank you. Thank you for your plan which is far beyond our understanding. Again, let us rejoice and be glad today because we know you are in control. Protect us all with Your hedge of protection and especially those who are in jail now. Keep them from being sent back to Haiti if that is Your will and allow families to stay united. We look to You for all guidance, wisdom and direction during this difficult time. We love you and ask all of this in Your Holy name, Jesus. Amen."

As we ended the prayer, I knew these precious children were in good hands and inwardly thanked Jesus for these girls giving their hearts to Blackwood. As I looked at the beautiful picture of love on the field, I couldn't help but wonder about those I knew were missing, Jean, Joseph, Junior, Davidson, Peterson. *Oh Lord I pray they are ok! Comfort your young men, Lord.*

* * * * * * *

As Michael and I stopped at the meat packing house, it was clear from the crowded parking lot of cars the Haitian people were indeed being detained inside the building.

"Michael, is it safe for us to be here?" I asked.

"Yes, but let's just stay in the car for now."

I watched the Defense Force and Police with their big guns slung across their shoulders, pacing in front of the large, open garage doors. The building was metal and perched on a foundation that required six or so steps to enter. I could see black bodies inside but not discern much else. The police were facing all the cars and watching us. One or two of the men had large cameras, too, and pointed them towards the cars taking pictures.

"Don't look up Amy and especially don't get out of the car," Michael said.

"Well what am I to do then? I can't see anything, and I want to know who was caught and how they are, Michael."

He looked at me like I was crazy. Thankfully I saw a Bahamian man I could go ask about the situation.

"Michael, can I go ask Watson? Please! Oh please!? We've sat here for so long now and nothing is happening. And I am worried, Michael!"

Finally, Michael relented. "Ok but make it quick Amy."

I approached Watson and he filled me in on the details. I ran back to the car to tell Michael.

"So, what did you find out?"

"Well, all our boys are in there. They are being questioned about their paperwork. They are determining and documenting who is legal and who is not. Basically, the entire community is in that meat packing house."

"All of them? They must be stuffed in there and so hot! There's only one door letting in light and air." Michael's voice was full of concern.

"Yeah, they probably are very hot, tired, thirsty and hungry." I continued, "I also spoke to the people in the car next to us and they told me some Haitians will go directly to Nassau to be processed in jail and then sent to Haiti. The others, which would be minors, will hopefully go home to Blackwood. Oh Michael, let's pray right now they don't send any of them back. That they would give them another chance to submit paperwork."

I have never prayed so hard before in my life but as I did, I knew God would answer that prayer. The Holy Spirit gave me peace and I felt calm as we finished. The time dragged on that day and we slowly began to see the Haitian people being released. One by one they left the big garage door and crept through the gate. Some entered cars and embraced awaiting friends and family crying and hugging one another. Others just quickly got in the cars and left as soon as they could. Finally, Davidson came out and gave us the story.

"Ms. Amy, you would not believe it, so many people got beaten, even if they had papers and were 'straight,' the police did not care. They chased us down; poor old Frantz he got trampled and beat really bad with the back of the rifle. He is all bloodied up."

"Oh Davidson, I am so sorry. But praise God you are here and safe. God answered our prayers, Davidson."

"Oh yea, you know, those police were really mean in there. They would not give us any water or food. Lots of babies and Moms were crying but people were praying real hard. You know Ms. Amy I was real glad to have Jesus in my heart. I have never prayed so hard in my life. And lots of other people were praying too. Lots were."

This story was repeated throughout the rest of the day while we picked up our beloved Haitian friends and carried them home to Blackwood. There were stories of prayers and cries lifted over and over again. People were scared and exhausted and still in shock, but most were grateful to be free. *Free indeed, but how long would it last?* I wondered.

As the gravity of the situation set in for me, I knew this battle was the Lord's and I was thankful for his intervention that Sunday in July of 2013. Most of the Haitian population was let go with a stern warning to file the necessary documents in order to stay in the country.

I would learn later that for someone like me that would be easy. I had a birth certificate and a passport as most people did who traveled internationally. But for a population of poor people who were just barely getting by financially, I discovered birth certificates were scarce and passports almost nonexistent. If a child had been raised in the Bahamas, they could not even file for a passport until they turned eighteen and then they had to be able to prove they were born in the Bahamas to stay legally. Otherwise, they would be required to return to Haiti until they had a passport with them.

Reaching home late in the day, Michael and I fell into bed. We explained to our questioning kids the severity of what had happened, but that God was always in control and always had the best plan. Our children were confused so we continued to explain that what might be thought of as "bad" in the world may be the very thing God would use for the Haitian people's "good."

"What do you mean Mama?" James asked.

"I mean if you look at Jesus, he died for us-for you and me. Because He died you and I would think that is something bad and sad but, it was only by Jesus' perfect, sinless life and death that we are able to have the best gift today which is a friendship with Him and eternal life in heaven someday!"

Little did I know this kingdom principle would soon transform our own lives as this first raid began a strict enforcement of existing laws for any illegal or refugee peoples within the Bahamas.

As the weeks went by it became apparent, we were sojourners ourselves. Just like them, we too were aliens in the land and had to continually fix our eyes and identity on Jesus alone. Freedom would come but not necessarily in the way we might have assumed. "So, if the Son sets free, you will be free indeed," from John 8:36 came to mind as I crawled into bed.

Tears came flooding out and I knew the pain of my precious Haitian friends. I had experienced it for myself and their pain was my pain. As I cried myself to sleep, I prayed I could navigate these surmounting difficulties we were now experiencing, *Oh, please Lord show us how to best help them with Your Gospel which is all they need, Lord. Amen.*

Chapter 17

Messiness of Everyday Life

...But you were washed, you were sanctified, you were justified in the name of the Lord Jesus Christ and by the Spirit of God.

1 Corinthians 6:11

After our presence and care during the painful incidence of the raid in Blackwood, the parents' and children's confidence in our family grew exponentially. Our Haitian friends saw how much we loved them by our actions aligning with our words. When things began to settle down within the community, there was a difference in their attitudes towards us. It was apparent they began to view us as people who would indeed help them. As soon as we could, we sought clarification with the Bahamian authorities, so we could begin to understand the process required for everyone to become legal and stay in the Bahamas. The laws were complicated and changing and expensive to obey. New processes such as an "Identification Permit" being required were costly and confusing but we knew God was allowing us to assist our friends since He kept on opening doors for us to do so. Onward we went.

Earning the community's trust allowed our ministry and the ministry's programs to grow. There was not only confidence in group settings, it was also assurance in us and the personal relationships we had with them. The first two boys, Jean and Davidson, who were baptized earlier in the summer, became Michael's good friends. He began discipling them, meeting and praying with them, and giving them godly counsel. Michael provided them with ministry opportunities and encouragement to become leaders within their own community so eventually they could lead others to Christ and teach them about Jesus.

"Multiplication, Amy, that is how Jesus lived out his ministry and so will we!" Michael said one Saturday.

"Remember Jesus' words, 'I will make you fishers of men?' Isn't it funny that I love to fish, and God used my passion and gift of fishing to provide for our family the first year in the Bahamas? Now He is allowing us to live by fishing for souls. Only God could think of such a thing," he said laughingly.

As with anything in life and being in community, there also came difficulties. One day Jean privately came to Michael and told us he had gotten his girlfriend pregnant. No one knew yet, and he sought Michael for counsel. Jean was embarrassed, ashamed and uncertain as to the next step.

As Michael told me about Jean's reaction to the pregnancy we prayed fervently. We asked God for the right scriptures to share with Jean and his girlfriend, Jesula, asking God to open their hearts to understanding this baby's life was made in the image of God.

Jesula was a newcomer to Blackwood and a new believer in Jesus as well. Right after she moved to the community and began dating Jean, we had invited her to come to an event where the gospel was preached every night. Anytime we could provide a chance for someone to hear the gospel, we gladly did.

During one of the messages on the last night of a four-day event, Jesula declared Jesus as Her Lord. We were thankful both she and Jean were believers and we now had the responsibility to teach them God's view of the pregnancy.

After a week of prayer and private conversations with Jean, Michael finally got Jean to bring Jesula over to visit. Michael and I had been intentionally praying for this opportunity and for our role in instructing them according to God's Word.

"Please come in, won't you?" I said as I welcomed them to our home.

After some small talk, we got down to the current situation. We learned they might want to keep the baby, but Jean had taken Michael's advice and told his parents about the pregnancy. They were not happy about it and did not want them to keep the baby. Unfortunately, Jesula and Jean were minors and were legally bound to listen to their parents. When I heard this information, I felt a strong urging to go to Ms. Merline, Jean's Mom, and intercede for this unborn child. I had become close to Merline and prayed God would use the situation for His glory and He would give me His wisdom and words. I quickly excused myself and said I would return shortly.

As I traveled over to Blackwood, I prayed passionately for God to change the parent's hearts. When I arrived about thirty minutes later, I went directly to Jean' parents' house and knocked on the door.

"Ms. Merline and Mr. Samuel, may I speak to you please?"

As they looked at one another, Jean's father motioned to Merline it was ok to speak with me outside. As we stepped out on the porch, I took her arm in mine.

"Ms. Merline, you know how much Michael and I love your entire family. All of your children have become a big part of our life, especially Jean. Michael in particular has become very close to Jean since last year. You

147

see how much time they spend together and how Jean is growing as a Christ-centered man. It's because of their relationship that Jean felt comfortable coming to Michael when he learned about the pregnancy. I hope you know we are here for Jean, Jesula and your whole family now."

She was looking down but looked up now and nodded her head.

"I have heard you are being disciplined at your church for Jean's sin of having this baby out of wedlock, and I know this is very hard for you. I want to plead with you to allow them to keep the baby. Jean tells us you think they are too young to have a baby now and you might even think they should abort the baby."

She looked up and nodded her head, quietly shaking *yes.*

As tears welled up in my eyes, I knew God was using me in the moment, so I took a deep breath and went on.

"Ms. Merline, I realize you might feel ashamed because you are a prominent woman in the church and a church leader, but this is not your sin. In fact, a baby is a blessing and this new life is a gift to Jean and Jesula and your whole family. It was a sin that they conceived the baby outside of wedlock, but God does not want them to abort the baby and cause more sin."

She hugged me, and we were swaying back and forth in her front yard, but she was not speaking. There was more I wanted to say.

"Please, please know that God forgives. He will forgive the fact that Jesula and Jean were intimate before marriage if they are willing to repent and confess it before Him."

I stopped for a moment as the tears were pouring out.

"Please Ms. Merline, I know you know the Bible. Think of Mary and Joseph and the result of baby Jesus. Mary was an unwed mother, too. I pray you will allow Jean and Jesula to have this baby. Michael and I will help with money and everything and anything."

Silence descended on the porch and Merline took my arms and embraced me as I was now sobbing. I laid my head on her shoulders and silently prayed, Oh Lord, please I beg you please, change her heart. Let this baby *live.*

"We will do whatever we can to help them with this baby, Ms. Merline, I promise," I told her.

I also knew a big concern was the financial commitment a pregnancy and baby demanded; money was scarce and so was work. There were other problems too that I knew Merline and her husband were considering such as their education; both Jean and Jesula would have to drop out of school. What kind of future would they have without high school diplomas? I still prayed silently, allowing the Lord and the abiding presence of the Holy Spirit to embrace us both. After some time, I finally let go and Ms. Merline said in her broken English that she would talk to Mr. Samuel.

"Does that mean you will allow the pregnancy?"

Hesitating, she looked at me and nodded her head *yes.* Now I squeezed her so tightly she even laughed a little and smiled with her head still somewhat looking down. *Victory Lord,* I thought! *Victory!*

After Ms. Merline went inside, I walked home on the trail that took me to the boat back to my island, crying every step of the way. I did not know if they were tears of sorrow or joy, but once the Holy Spirit gave me an inward peace, I knew the baby would be born. I continued to pray fervently that Mr. Samuel would now agree with his wife about keeping the baby.

When I arrived home, Michael was ending the discussion with Jean and Jesula that I had abruptly left. He told me he'd shown them in the Bible that having sex before marriage is a sin when you call yourself a follower of Jesus. But if they understood this and sought God's forgiveness, He was faithful and just to forgive them. Michael also asked them about marriage. Did they love one another and want to make a lifelong commitment? Privately, Jean had told us he did want to marry Jesula, but they had not spoken about it together yet. Michael and I hoped they did, and he presented the idea, showing them the mystery of marriage was in God bringing them together.

When I entered the conversation, I heard them tell Michael they would think about marriage. I added my own thoughts, saying that each life is made in God's image, and although God created sex for pleasure it is within the confines of marriage. Lastly, Michael and I reminded them the Holy Spirit indwells the "temple," our body, and aborting the baby would defile it. We pleaded with them to not go down this treacherous path of disobedience because it would produce another sin of loss of life.

By the end of our time together, Jean and Jesula had repented from immorality and were determined to have the baby if their parents agreed. They also wanted to get married and Michael and I rejoiced with them through our tears. More rejoicing came later that evening after Jesula and Jean had returned and spoken to Jean's parents. Jean phoned to tell Michael they had agreed—Jesula could have the baby!

I was overjoyed because I knew a new season of helping with the pregnancy would be next. I thanked God for the confidence He had given me to obey Him. When I prayed about sharing with Ms. Merline, God had taken me right to 1 John 1:5–7 which reads, "This is the message we have heard from him and proclaim to you, that God is light, and in him is no darkness at all. If we say we have fellowship with him while we walk in darkness we lie and do not practice the truth. But if we walk in the light, as he is the light, we have fellowship with one another, and the blood of Jesus his Son cleanses us from all sin." Light always conquers darkness and I was thankful for God leading hearts to obedience by the authority of His word.

* * * * * * *

Once the parents had agreed, I wanted to get Jesula in for an examination as soon as possible so there would be no uncertainty about rescinding their decision. The soonest appointment was three days later at the local and only clinic on the island.

Together, Jesula and I bravely entered the clinic. I was again stepping into a new period of unknowing. The head nurse informed me under Bahamian law Jesula could not stay in school if she was pregnant. The only possibility for schooling was to be accepted into the teen girl pregnancy school in Nassau. But Nassau was a whole other island away. *Where would she live? How would she survive?* I began to wonder.

The nurse went on to say that not just anyone can attend this school but must have a referral before acceptance. She told us that Haitians were not typically allowed as this is a Bahamian country and the funds to go to this privileged school were paid by the Bahamian government and thus, they were used for Bahamian teenagers.

Oh Lord, please, please, show me what to do, I prayed silently. The nurse said she would try her best, but the process would begin with a call to the school in Nassau and to see if there would be space for Jesula. I would have to make that call myself.

"Day after day, all I get is a busy signal, Michael. What do I do? I can't get through." I was getting very anxious.

I went back to the Nurse who also tried to call and in bewilderment said she did not know what to do either. We were wasting precious time as the end of July was approaching and school would be commencing September first. Finally, I made one final trip back to the clinic and the Director of all the island clinics was there for that day. I decided to speak to him in person.

"Hello, Mrs. Boykin, I am Mr. Knowles, how can I help you today?"

After explaining the situation, he said we would need proper identification to enroll Jesula and since she did not have any ID, this would be a problem.

"Oh, Mr. Knowles, please help us," I pleaded.

During our conversation I noticed something about him was different. I was beginning to wonder why he was nicer and more helpful than any Bahamian I had ever met. He was attempting to help a pregnant Haitian girl, which was way out of the norm for a Bahamian.

After asking about his family I discovered his wife had been my children's teacher at school.

"Oh, thank you Jesus," I said under my breath.

I told him how much my children loved his wife as their teacher and how thankful I was for her involvement in their local church. These were some of things I remembered as she also had a daughter who had been in Marley's class at school. *Wow Jesus, thank you, thank you. For only you could connect the dots like this for me and Jesula,* I whispered.

Once we figured out the connections Mr. Knowles went above and beyond meeting us at another island and helping us get the proper identification for Jesula to attend school. He found the Principal's personal number and called and enrolled Jesula immediately. And just like that God opened the door wide open for Jesula to go to school.

The enemy was not about to give up so easily, though. As soon as this news made its way back to Blackwood, problems arose. After we had made it through such a big hurdle, I did not expect to encounter more opposition, but we did. As Jesula and I were celebrating her new beginning we went over to tell Jean and his family. Jesula had a mother and sister in Blackwood too, but she spent most of her nights at Jean's house sleeping on the sofa in the living room. Jesula's mother Fabienne was hardly ever home and when she was, she was rarely coherent. I got along well with her because she was the first woman I personally helped when our ministry moved over to Blackwood. She was one of the women displaced from Apea to Blackwood over a year ago and I had secured a mattress for her bed, and gave her money to buy supplies to build herself a tiny, one-bedroom house. I hoped this previous relationship would help me and Jesula as we walked directly to her house to share the news with her Mom.

When we walked up, we saw Fabienne sitting with several men smoking under the tree outside her house. It smelled illegal, but I was not about to question her. Fabienne was known as a prostitute and a drunk, but I needed her help in order to help Jesula. "Oh Lord, please give me Your wisdom," I said inwardly.

"Hi Mom," Jesula said.

"Um, hi," she said, sort of throwing her head back, her eyes almost rolling back into her head.

"Oh no," I thought to myself

"Mom, Ms. Amy has gotten me into the school for pregnant girls in Nassau. Can I go?"

"How ya payin fer it?" Fabienne slurred.

"Ms. Amy and some others who have contributed are giving me the money."

"Ms. Amy, give me the money and I will take her myself," stammered Fabienne.

"You know she has to have my approval too don't ya? She can't go by herself ya know, Ms. Amy, she a minor."

"Yes, I know Ms. Fabienne, but I want to make sure she is in a good living environment and can get to school," I replied, trying to persuade her to relent.

"Oh, don worries, just give me the money and I can do that." Fabienne could barely get the words out now.

I did not know what to do because she was correct in saying Jesula needed her permission for school and they did not have money. I also knew she could take the money and use it on alcohol. *Oh Lord, please help me*, I prayed.

"Ok, Ms. Fabienne, let me talk to Mr. Michael and get back to you."

As I hugged Jesula good bye I told her to pray and it would be ok. But I told her to hurry home to Jean's family's house now and stay with them. *Oh Lord, will it really be okay? Please help!* I walked down the trail to the ferry which would take me back to Spanish Wells, praying all the way.

* * * * * * *

God ultimately prevailed, and I went with Jesula to Nassau to enroll her in school. God also gave her an opportunity to live with a friend of her mother's. The necessary money for food and transportation was supplied through the ministry and friends with whom we had shared the story. God had given us the ability "...both to will and to work according to His good pleasure," just as Philippians 2:13 describes.

Although I was cautious about Jesula's living situation, once we arrived in Nassau, I was relieved when I met her caretaker. Madeline was a sweet old woman who had taken in a young boy T.J. and was raising him. Her house, although in a bad part of town, was nicely kept and I felt peaceful as I hugged Jesula goodbye for the time being. Jehovah Jireh, the Lord of provision and protection, was with her.

In the end, almost a year and a half year after Jean had first approached Michael, a beautiful baby boy named Justin was born on November 15, 2014. God taught us a lot about seriousness of the God-given position he had placed us in and the grave responsibilities we have in proclaiming how to live by His Word. The reality of His calling and His ministry was not to be taken lightly as we had experienced the power of the gospel, redemptive love, and how it worked to show God's glory.

Justin's new life was proof of that.

Chapter 18

A New Foundation

Surely the Lord has given all the land into your hands...

Joshua 2:24

THE WAY

I awoke in the morning astonished by the vivid memories from the night before. I'd never been able to recall details from a dream like this. I also never had a dream where I knew God was instructing me to do something so specific, but it did not surprise me. In fact, it only made me excited. God was constantly revealing Himself as the God of new beginnings like he did with Jean and Jesula's pregnancy. Whether it was the birth of a baby or the birth of His church, God wanted our family to experience Him in His fullness.

When God's ministry expanded into Blackwood, we wanted to build a church for the people because they had none, yet God had never opened a door to construct a building.

Still, our work was growing, and Michael and I knew our friends needed a place to congregate regularly. Although the soccer field housed the basketball court and pavilion, it was a challenging place to gather. Meaningful conversations with goats roaming around you proved difficult. Kids running in different directions while a basketball game commenced presented problems while talking about Jesus on the pavilion.

We could also see God wanted a church to be a place for adults and children to gather together to worship and learn about Jesus. It was clear the field would not hold the multiplication of young adults and children; God wanted His kingdom to expand into the adults. Our role was to be carriers of Jesus' Word to all the Haitian people in the community; especially those who never came to the field and the adults who only came for special events.

Other problems manifested without a building as well. Our ESL adult classes had continued in the pavilion but lost steam because the outdoor conditions were harsh.. Now I clearly understood. We were ambassadors of God's message laid out in Romans 10:14–15; "How then will they call on him in whom they have not believed? And how are they to believe in him of whom they have never heard? And how are they to hear without someone preaching? And how are they to preach unless they are sent? As it is written," How beautiful are the feet of those who preach the good news!""

We had prayed and fasted and even went so far as to search out land, but God had not yet answered that prayer. Instead He had given us Scripture from Habakkuk 2:3, "For the vision is yet for the appointed time.

It hastens toward the goal and it will not fail. Though it tarries, wait for it; For it will certainly come, it will not delay."

Here it was May of 2014 and God was telling us it was finally time, *His* "appointed time;" and the directive was crystal clear.

Overjoyed with His presence, I quickly turned and tapped Michael.

"Honey, wake up."

Michael leaned over sleepily and tried to listen.

"You will never believe it, but I had a dream last night and God showed me where to build His church for the Blackwood community."

"What?" I now had Michael's attention and he sat up in bed.

"What do you mean? We never have gotten an answer about building a church."

"Yes, I know but that's changed. I never had a dream telling me it is time to build a church building! God showed me the land and told me to build there."

"Michael, I don't know where it is, but I will once I see it."

In my dream I had seen an overgrown, fenced in property with the remains of a concrete slab and banana trees growing out of the middle. I knew if we went looking in the Blackwood neighborhood, I'd know the property when I saw it.

Elated with His presence, I snuggled up to Michael and thanked God for this answered prayer. *Our mission was going to be complete with a church,* I thought to myself. Suddenly the Holy Spirit let me know building a church for this community was the main reason God brought us to the Bahamas. As I lay in bed that morning, I pondered how God was using our American family to now build His church building; a permanent, everlasting home for His people. With no directives but from the Holy Spirit and God's Word, He had led us on a journey to this very moment.

I searched Scripture for confirmation. Would God really use people like us who were untrained, inexperienced and unqualified? I thought back to our Austin church's strategy to send us to Turkey. It included training classes, a sending agency and raising support. But as their plan unfolded, I had significant reservations about their vision; I did not find scripture to support their ideas. Some things resonated from the church's plan but none were as black and white as they mandated. Remembering Paul was a tentmaker and supported himself much of his ministry gave me confidence to study the Word again.

When I looked again, this time, I found as the disciples were fasting and praying "...the Holy Spirit said, "Set apart for me Barnabas and Saul for the work to which I have called them," from in Acts 13:2.

I debated with God again in my prayer closet, *Ok, You did give us confirmation from our Mission Pastors to come here. Our small group prayed over us and sent us out blessing us. But it was You, only You, who "called" us. We did as you asked according to Scripture. Lord, it may have taken four years to become obedient, but we did leave everything and follow You. It has been for Your glory that we have a ministry and have been used as vessels to bring people into your kingdom family. Now they need a permanent home. I know Matthew 16:18 says, "And I tell you, you are Peter, and on this rock, I will build my church, and the gates of Hades will not overcome it," that we are chosen ambassadors like Peter and that You, Jesus, are the "rock." All of this makes sense to me, but God, I'm not sure I have the courage to complete this task.*

I sat quietly for some time waiting for a response. Finally, the Holy Spirit showed me the phrase, "I will build my church." Staring at it, God illuminated what He meant by explaining it was HIS job to build the church, not mine. I thanked God over and over again for alleviating the pressure; the outcome of "His" church was just that—"His" outcome.

God would bring the clergy, the members and establish the bylaws; all we had to do was construct the building. I laughed now thinking the evangelizing and disciplemaking that had occurred for years now was actually the hardest part! The easier task of construction was all that was left. We knew a lot about that since that was what we did in Austin! *Oh God, you are so, so GOOD! I simply have to be willing and obedient.* God had chosen our family and brought us this far and I knew He would complete the task; we just had to step into this new phase. Confident, I arose to begin my day in search of finding the land.

I got dressed in a hurry, excited to look for the land God had shown me. It was a blistering hot day and we had a mission team serving with us at the time. Once I arrived in Blackwood with the team, I began telling the details of my dream to a few of the participants. I was in mid-conversation when I looked up and there it was; the property just as I had seen in it. It was amazing because of its proximity to the soccer field, basketball court and pavilion. There it was, right across the main road from where we shared life every day with the Blackwood community. Ecstatic and thankful I raced over to Michael and hugged him tightly, "Look, there it is!

Praising God, we walked over to the property and it *did* have an old slab with banana trees in the middle! Michael and I laughed and hugged more and then prayed thanking the Lord for His perfect timing and plan.

I realized why we hadn't seen it—the dilapidated fence with vines engulfing it had hidden the overgrown property and it just blended into the rest of the scenery. Although the land was vacated, we knew since there were the remnants of a foundation that the land was owned by someone. It would be our task to find the owner.

"Michael, how will we find who holds the title to the land?" I asked.

"I don't know, but it's probably one of the farmers we see driving up and down the road," he responded.

As we began investigating, we found out a house was on the property about 10 years ago, but it had burned down. We also discovered that under Bahamian law, the Blackwood area was "commonage land" and cannot be owned by anyone. The land is for the use of the Bahamians and provides a means for them to be able to farm and make a living from agricultural professions. Only they can claim the land. Over the years the Bahamians had seen a business opportunity just like they had in Apea, except this land was technically not owned by Bahamians, simply claimed by them. A Bahamian would mark and maintain allotted boundaries with fruit trees for farming. Not all the land was used in this way, so some savvy farmers allowed the Haitians to build residences on the property in exchange for work or money or both.

Michael and I spent two days asking the various farmers who frequented the main road of Blackwood if they knew anything about the property.

THE WAY

We found out a Bahamian man, a Mr. Cartwright, held the title and was actually someone we knew of, but had never formally met or spoken to.

That night before bed Michael and I prayed for direction about how to approach him and rehearsed our speech to one another about what we would say. On and on we practiced, thinking we were surely going to receive rejection from him. Certainly, he would not take kindly to us using the property to build a Haitian church.

I had been cautious when speaking to local people about our ministry because most Bahamians did not embrace our love for the Haitian people. Most of the locals considered them an unwanted intrusion in their country; a people who illegally had migrated to the Bahamas and now took away much needed jobs. In some cases, this was true but for most and especially the ones we taught and lived with, they were the first generation of children being raised in the Bahamas.

The next morning as we headed over to Blackwood I was surprised when Michael nudged me as we exited the ferry at the dock.

"There he is!" whispered Michael.

"You go ask him, Amy!"

"Me?"

"Michael, I thought you were going to talk to him!"

"He's walking towards us, what should I say again? I'm too nervous, I can't Michael; not now anyway,"

Michael shoved me forward saying, "Hurry, just introduce yourself, I will follow up later."

Mr. Cartwright now had to stop as I was standing squarely in front of him.

"Um, Mr. Cartwright, hello. My name is Amy Boykin. My family and I are the ones who work with the community in Blackwood sharing the love of Jesus."

"Yes, yes, I know who you are," he replied.

"Well, would there be a time my husband and I could sit down with you and discuss our vision for building a church in the community? We saw your property and thought maybe we could work out something with you to build on it."

"You want to build a church there?" he responded. "Well, I do appreciate all that you do here in the community."

Oh no, I thought, waiting for the "However...." to come next.

But he continued, "You are welcome to do that. I would be glad for you to use the property any way you would like."

I was dumbfounded and stammered, "But don't we need to meet to talk more about this?

"No, no, like I said, I am thankful for what you folks do and you can use it any way you want to. Just let me know how I can be of help. I have to be moving on now," he said and briskly walked away.

Surprised, I stammered back, "Ok, thank you sir, thank you so much. Does this mean we can call you?"

By now he was some distance ahead. I turned and said again more loudly, "Don't we need to go over more details about how all this work, Mr. Cartwright?"

Pausing, he looked back at me, "Oh yes, no problem. Just ring my house and we can get it sorted out. My wife is usually at home, Marcie is her name."

I was shocked this man believed in us; believed in our work and would allow us to do this. I ran to catch up with Michael who was now far ahead and told him what had happened. We were in disbelief. To live in a country that does not embrace Haitians and for a man we did not know to affirm our plan was amazing. It showed us this whole idea was only from God. He alone is faithful to complete what he begins. Again, and again, He was teaching us how as we were obedient to His leading, He would open the doors, we just merely had to walk through them.

The Holy Spirit reminded me how we had already been down a similar road when we built the basketball court. That land also had been claimed

THE WAY

by a Bahamian and after a local negotiated on our behalf, he relented and allowed us to build the court in lieu of using it for farming. In that case, we had to pay the man several thousand dollars for the opportunity to build, regardless it was God's hand at work. Mr. Jones, who did not attend church and told us he was not fond of the Haitians, still was used by God, working with us to provide a simple thing like a basketball court. Later that evening, Michael called Mr. Cartwright to discuss how we would receive the land. Since we were Americans and not Bahamian, we could not be recipients of this "crown land" or government property. But as Michael spoke to him, he asked if we could have our local Bahamian church be the recipients, since our ministry was a partner with them. We would assume all details of the building project such as raising funds to furnish it and overseeing the construction, but legally the new Blackwood church would become a church plant of our local Church in Spanish Wells. This allowed the new church to be completely legal under Bahamian law.

Michael and I were amazed at how God was teaching us His ways. 2 Corinthians 9:8 became a reality, "And God is able to make all grace abound to you, so that having all sufficiency in all things at all times, you may abound in every good work." He had divinely influenced Mr. Cartwright's heart and now the ministry was growing and finding favor.

The paperwork and permitting process only took six short weeks, which was perfect timing since a large mission team was coming from Mississippi in June. Quickly those weeks went by with the team arriving just in time for the new construction to commence.

Working side by side in the scorching heat with the team and our Haitian family, we began the tedious process of collecting rocks of all shapes and sizes for the new church foundation. I realized how God was amazingly intentional as I thought of who Jesus is. Matthew 21:42 records, "Jesus said to them, 'Have you never read in the Scriptures, "The stone which the builders rejected has become the chief cornerstone: the Lord has done this, and it is marvelous in our eyes'?"

I laughed as I tried to tell one of our mission participants how cool God is.

"Can you believe God gave us the ministry name, "The Living Stone Ministry" and here we are laying the foundation for His new church with these stones from Blackwood?"

"Yeah, not to mention, didn't you tell us on the first night that the Scripture for the ministry name meant we believers are "stones" with a little "s" who follow Jesus who is the capital "S?"

"Oh Susie," I said laughing now. "That's even better! You are so right!"

"Yeah, when you first said that, I was thinking to myself about when Jesus says He is the "chief cornerstone" like you said a while ago. Now I remember what you explained. God truly is always working, isn't He?"

Through many conversations like these I found God working in each small detail of my life. I was sharing with a new friend from the mission team she was also a "stone" like me and I needed her to help build God's kingdom. We all needed Jesus as our anchor and foundation.

By end of summer the foundation was ready to be poured, but most importantly God was building His everlasting, permanent church in Blackwood.

SECTION FOUR

FULLNESS

*By this my Father is glorified, that you bear much fruit
and so prove to be my disciples. As the Father has loved
me, so I have loved you. Abide in my love. If you keep my
commandments you will abide in my love, just as I have kept
my Father's commandments and abide in his love. These
things I have spoken to you, that my joy may be in you, and
that your joy may be full.*

John 15:8–11

Chapter 19

Pressing On – His Will Be Done

But I say to you who hear, Love your enemies, do good to those who hate you, bless those who curse you, pray for those who abuse you.

Luke 6:27–28

Opposition came immediately once we broke ground on God's church building. Gratefully, as the door to construct the building opened, God had led me to study Nehemiah from the Old Testament to learn God's leadership skills and study the opponent's strategies. He was teaching me opposition was a key part of expanding His kingdom. During the re-building of the temple Nehemiah faced anger, mockery, sarcasm, threats and intimidation, just to name a few of the enemy's tactics. Those same age-old tricks were being unleashed on me, my family and the ministry. I was about to discover the enemy was kicking his game up a notch and this was only the beginning. Having a church building meant eternity was fixed for Christ. The enemy also knew this and was not going down without an all-out war.

I was standing with the new mission team next to the dock when, "Honk, Honk, Honk!" was all I heard as we bowed in our prayer circle.

I lifted my head and opened my eyes to see what was going on as my hand was yanked to move over. Jerking my body sideways I was pulled out of the way and saw a truck coming right towards me and the mission team. The driver came to a stop. An old Bahamian man with a cane exited an old pick-up truck. He had tried to drive into the prayer circle but stopped short of hitting a person and now was hobbling towards me yelling, "Get your van out of the way, you're in my parking spot!"

I walked directly toward him as he continued shouting at me.

"Who do you think you are!? You can't do this!" He let me have it.

Pointing his cane in the air he limped towards me, red-faced and shout-ing, "Who told you could build in Blackwood? And better yet a church for monkeys?!"

He continued his obscenities interspersed with racial slurs. The mission team stood watching in complete silence as I ushered the nameless man to the side of the dock, praying inwardly.

I could hardly contain myself as the anger rose within me toward this man I had never spoken to in my life. Since he would not calm down, I began praying out loud, looking directly at the ground as he shouted in my face. Spit was spewing from his mouth and I could feel the heat of his breath, but the Holy Spirit kept saying to me, *Amy, do not respond. Do not respond! Keep praying. The Lord is with you, He is with you.*

Amongst the yelling I heard him repeatedly ask how I could build on Bahamian land. That I was American and could not do this and he was going to make sure and stop it.

Finally, I spoke.

"Please call the People's Church and speak to our lead Pastor, Mr. Damon Rolle to confirm that I do have legal permission to build in Blackwood," I directed him.

"Na, there's no way. You are lyin," he accused.

Somehow, I was able to stand and look him squarely in the eye.

"I do have approval to build because we are doing so under The People's Church of the Bahamas. Our ministry is a part of this congregation. This new church plant in Blackwood is an extension of The People's Church in title and deed."

He looked at me cock-eyed and started mumbling to himself. Not only did he look like a mad man, but he acted and sounded like one too. As he walked away, he turned and shook his finger at me taunting me, "You won't hear the last of this, young lady."

More mumbling followed but it was hard to discern. A friend who had been standing by my side said, "Amy, he just said he hates Americans, Pastors and churches but most of all Haitians."

"What?" I said, trembling.

Although I had tried my best to be courageous in front of this high school mission team, I was really scared, and my shaking revealed it. My Bahamian girlfriend Cherise was the only local who would help me from time to time and I was grateful she was with me since Michael was out of town. She patted my back and said, "Take deep breaths, I will take the team and walk them up the trail to Blackwood."

Mr. Wilson, one of the adult leaders on the mission team, approached me, somewhat shaken himself.

"That man ran into your ministry van intentionally when we would not stop praying and move out of the way of his truck, Amy."

"Oh, really?" I said.

"I am so sorry, Mr. Wilson," replied.

"Sorry for me? Oh no, I am sorry for you!" he shot back.

I walked over and just stared at our van and said, "Well, at least we are all ok. Don't worry, I will let the local church know about what happened and maybe they can help."

As the old man walked away from me toward the ferry, I wondered if the Bahamian church would really help. Up until this point their assistance had been sponsorship for the ministry but other than that they kept to themselves. As our ministry was under their direct leadership, I was curious to see if they would stand with us and confront this man about his comments. I also questioned if they would address this issue once I told them or allow this crazy man to come to them first. *Lord, let your will be done. Amen.*

Thankfully no one was hurt, and the team was excited to get into Blackwood to begin work on the church. The lovingkindness of the Haitian children they had met was infectious and made it easy to want to help them. As I watched the team begin the trek up the trail, I tried to process the events and calm myself down.

Ok, Amy, it is clear the team has no idea this spiritual attack is directly correlated to the church we're building. Michael's with the kids at the softball tournament in Nassau which makes this an even better opportunity to come against me, as I am alone leading this team, I reasoned.

"But God," was all I heard now. If it hadn't been for God... *Ok, yes, yes, Lord, I hear You. You are in charge and You will never leave me or forsake me. You haven't yet and won't. Thank you, Jesus. Amen.*

After I gave myself this little pep talk, I started walking to catch up with the group. It was unfortunate Michael was gone but I felt confident I could handle it with God. I had already begun to witness the gospel's agitating power against "the rulers, against the authorities, against the cosmic powers over this present darkness, against the spiritual forces of evil in the heavenly places." the Apostle Paul writes about in the book of Ephesians.

I had to separate this man in the truck from the evil that was brewing within him and directed at me. As I caught up to the team on the trail, I prayed silently the armor of God verses from Ephesians chapter six over the team participants, the Blackwood neighborhood and myself and my family. The Holy Spirit had taken control of my fearful flesh in that confrontation and I was grateful. I was thankful we were all safe and indebted to the Holy Spirit, who had led me to not dishonor Jesus, since I had wanted to scream back at the man. I prayed for him instead and asked God for strength and courage to continue to love him just like I did the Haitian people. *He's not evil, Satan is. The darkness of this world uses people and blinds them to the truth of the gospel,* I thought. *Pray a blessing for him Amy, pray a blessing,* I said to myself.

Unfortunately, this was not the first time we saw locals who were unhappy about loving our neighbors. One Bahamian friend of Michael's had said to him privately, "Man, you know we all think it's great what you are doing and all, but you don't have to take it *this far."*

I realized that even when you think those closest to you will support you, I couldn't be completely sure of the Bahamian church's help. God was showing us we were sent to share what it means to live for Jesus to the Haitians *and* Bahamians. As I thought back to the comment I had made to Mr. Wilson, the mission team leader, I pondered if our sponsoring church *would* intervene in the ministry's defense. Up until this point their assistance had been sponsorship for the ministry but other than that they kept their outreach confined to Spanish Wells. I wondered if they would help because I had experienced what we were up against first hand.

I thought back to an event from a few short weeks earlier. It was early evening and we had gathered as we always did with our mission team to eat. Except on this night I had invited some of our local Bahamian church leadership to join us for supper. Michael and I regularly invited locals from the community to join in, so they could participate with us in the Holy Spirit's movement. As I sat at the end of the table with the mission team leaders and the two locals, the conversation lulled, and the church elder fixed his stern gaze on me.

"Amy, you know there are a lot of people who don't like what you do."

Unfortunately for me, Michael was at the other end of the table. As the man's eyes locked with mine, the peace of the Holy Spirit resonated through me as I confidently answered him back, "Yes I do know and that is the very reason Jesus sent me and my family not only to the Haitians but to Spanish Wells too."

In the heat of the moment, I had just opened my mouth and the words came out clearly and humbly. The Holy Spirit had spoken that night, not me.

When we finally made it home that night, I told Michael about my conversation. We searched Scripture and saw Jesus' comforting instructions to his disciples in Luke 21:14–15, "But make up your mind not to worry beforehand how you will defend yourselves. For I will give you words and wisdom that none of your adversaries will be able to resist or contradict." The words mirrored my dinner table experience.

Looking more intently, scripture was now coming to life for me as I read about the criticism Paul, Timothy and Titus endured in their ministries. Titus 1:16 summarized many in our community, "They profess to know God, but they deny him by their works…" As God's ministry was bearing much fruit for His kingdom, jealousy set in just as it did when the apostle Paul warned the believers in Galatia saying, "Let us not become conceited, provoking one another, envying one another." It seemed that many of the entitled locals resented the way our mission teams loved the Haitian people and the way the Haitians returned that love.

This attitude was becoming more apparent as the Bahamian believers resisted the truth of the grace which Paul summarizes in Galatians 5:13–15, "For you were called to freedom brothers. Only do not use your freedom as an opportunity for the flesh, but through love serve one another. For the whole law is fulfilled in one word: "You shall love your neighbor as yourself." But if you bite and devour one another, watch out that you are not consumed by one another." Earlier in chapter 3 Paul reminds fellow believers that their unified love of one another comes from justification in Christ alone. Verse 28 says, "There is neither Jew nor Greek, there is neither slave nor free, there is no male and female, for you are all one in Christ Jesus."

God continued to teach us that He is sufficient to sustain us through these criticisms. If the religious community was going to persecute us as happened in Paul's day, Christ alone could provide friendship with like-minded people who came to serve as mission team participants. Jesus was quite capable to build His kingdom if we were willing to obey. Clearly, scriptures such as, "In this world you will have trouble but take heart I have overcome the world," in John 16:33 were becoming a reality for Michael and me. We were learning we were different and that we had to continue to be different to show who Jesus is and how He lives. "Let your light shine before men in such a way that they may see your good works, and glorify your Father who is in heaven." became a daily reality to us as Jesus said to his disciples in Matthew 5:16. Outwardly local people embraced our mission but when push came to shove few were willing to participate on a regular basis. It was fine if we reached out to the Haitians, but our Bahamian church friends were reluctant. We would repeatedly extend invitations to help us with the ministry, but few Bahamians saw the necessity to serve the least of these in the community. Although there were some who did help in various ways, most of them were happy to let us do the work.

Other persecution was also beginning to come with our kids at school. Suzelynda had now been permanently living with us for the year and many of the locals just backed away, especially the children. Some of them no longer played with my kids or would be allowed to stay overnight at our house. Others would make fun of Suze right in front of her and my own kids. Quickly our family was being taught that truly following Jesus has consequences. Every new chapter afforded us a lesson we could thank God for and we used it all for His glory.

"See, kids if we were not doing something for the Lord, we would not be facing opposition. Remember God sees success differently than the world sees it," Michael said one night at our dinner devotion. "Stay strong in the Lord and remember to always show His mercy, grace and love."

"Dad, I did that today," Marley said.

"What did you do Marley?" Michael asked.

"One of my friends was asking me why I was being nice to her even though she always cheated off my papers during tests and talked behind my back. I told her I only did that because it's exactly what Jesus would do."

Michael looked at me for a response; I had none except to encourage Marley by saying, "Praise the Lord, Marley and keep up the great work of living like Jesus."

As I rejoiced in my daughter's bravery and for accepting this as part of following Jesus, I inwardly wondered if she and my other children would be able to have a "normal" childhood. I prayed they would be able to grow up feeling love not only from their family but from others claiming to follow Jesus.

The next morning as I was praying, the Counselor, the Holy Spirit, whispered, *Read John 14:15, Amy.* I opened my Bible to, "If you love me, you will keep my commandments." I shut my eyes to focus on what He was saying I heard the Holy Spirit answer my prayer from the night before, *Amy, what is "normal" in the world is not necessarily "normal" as a follower of Jesus. Jesus was different and constantly created commotion because He called people to obedience.*

Time and again I thanked the Holy Spirit for this revelation and thought about how my children were growing up understanding how to live out their faith and love like we are called to over and over again in Scripture. I was glad to know verses like Philippians 1:27 where Paul instructs the church, "Only conduct yourselves in a manner worthy of the gospel of Christ, so that whether I come and see you or remain absent, I will hear of you that you are standing firm in one spirit, with one mind striving together for the faith of the gospel." This had become a truth in my family's life.

****

Even though some of the locals were backing away from me and my family, God was blessing us by sending people who would shower us with love.

"Mom, I cannot wait for Amber to come back!" Marley said one afternoon.

"Today they all arrive!" Josie chimed in.

"Please remember to get us out of school early so we can go pick them up at the dock!" my girls continued.

We were blessed with a group of college age girls and boys who, because of their powerful experience while on mission, wanted to come back and serve with us again. The first summer nine college students served as interns and this number grew over the course of the following years. We would gratefully accept their assistance in the day to day operations with the mission teams and ministry. The three girls who had witnessed the first Blackwood raid became some of our closest allies and friends. The Lord was building relationships and furthering His plan through people He had connected us to for His mission.

Not only did God provide friendship, love, support and fellowship for the Haitian people through these students but they also showed the same to our children, Michael and me. Since that first summer was a mutual success, we asked them to come back throughout the entire duration of our mission in Blackwood.

Eventually I organized the ministry's first official Intern mission trip. These returnees put together Christmas gifts for the kids just as we had done the year prior with my friend Ann. My family was so excited, and my girls anxiously awaited the young adults' arrival. God was bringing a bit of "home" right to us in the Bahamas. We were grateful for the mutual affection for one another and ultimately these original interns who served with us the first Summer became like our own children. We treated them like family and shared all we had with them emotionally, spiritually and financially. They also gave all they had to our family and the ministry showering us and the Haitian community with gifts and love. It was a beautiful portrait of what the early church looks like fellowshipping and loving one another, displaying Christ's glory as stated in Acts 2: 44, "And all who believed were together and had all things in common."

These visits gave our family great joy since we could speak freely about our passion for the Haitian people and God's growing ministry. This was the very thing our lives were centered on and we relished our common perspective. These times together and subsequent trips over the following summers and Christmases inspired us to press on and pray for the locals who were persecuting us.

Even amidst sufferings, we persevered, and God protected us mightily. His hand of favor was upon us and He alone continued to grow His presence. We were keenly aware we were to be used as His instruments and be at His disposal. As problems arose, we would seek His wisdom in the Word. It seemed as if after each passing difficulty God would send us encouragement and blessings in the form of teams and donations. Quickly God's new residence, the church, was taking shape and by the end of the year we were grateful to be making progress. We were also grateful for our

FULLNESS – Pressing On – His Will Be Done

local church's continued partnership regardless of their stance on loving others as well as the few local friends who helped us with the ministry when they could.

We appreciated the many mission teams who worked hard on the church building and for the continued growth of our own family. We were still living out the dream God had instilled so many years prior. It was funny how I never had any idea what that dream really was. What I did know was it was not the life I had experienced, the so-called "American Dream." The 'more' I initially prayed for from the Prayer of Jabez was what God had unfolded by faith in obedience to Christ. Sending our family into the unknown allowed us to truly learn who He is and become centered in Jesus and Him alone. Now we were teaching and being taught simultaneously how to walk lovingly like Jesus.

Yet, along with the blessings came rejection as well. Little did I know I was about to face my biggest disappointment yet.

Chapter 20

Suze's Rejection –
An Unlikely Answer
to Prayer

*If the world hates you, you know that it has
hated Me before it hated you.*

John 15:18

It was 10:40 on Christmas Eve when we heard knocking on our front door.

"Who could be coming by this late?" I asked Michael.

I opened the door and was shocked to see the Newbolds standing there. They were local Bahamians and Suzelynda's sponsorship family.

Upon Suze's eighteenth birthday, God had miraculously moved upon the hearts of this local couple. They loved Suze and had a daughter, Anastasia, who was close to her as well. More importantly, they knew once Suzelynda turned eighteen she had to work to live in the country. Anastasia had approached Suze earlier in the Summer telling her that her family wanted her to work for them. They would apply for a work permit to sponsor her to stay and have a job. Suze's sponsorship was like The People's Church sponsorship for our ministry; it allowed our family to reside and work legally within the Bahamas.

"Amy, we are so sorry to come by so late, but we had to show you this letter."

I could see they were upset and quickly read the letter which was addressed to them and Suzelynda. It was a rejection denying Suze access to work in the Bahamas.

Rumors had been circulating throughout the summer that people were going to call the government as soon as Suze turned 18 to say she had been living with us illegally. Many locals wanted Suze gone as they did most of the other Haitians, but God was always one step ahead in His plan. He had already secured the answer by the Newbold's sponsorship, or that's what we all assumed until this fateful night.

The letter related that Suze was denied the work permit and must vacate the Bahamas immediately. With tears streaming down my face there was nothing I could say. I was stunned. I did not expect Suze to be denied. I thanked the Newbold's and hugged them goodnight.

I returned to bed and poured my heart out to Michael.

"What are we going to do?" I asked.

We sat there bewildered and began to pray, asking for God's wisdom and His way for Suzelynda. After three and a half years of her being a part of our family it would be devastating to see her leave. I could not

177

imagine my life without her; she was always at my side and we all loved her very much. As we prayed and sought the Lord, we knew of only one answer... she must return to her home country of Haiti.

Although this whole situation seemed terribly unfair, it was the law. And if we were to live and reside in a country, any country, we felt strongly that we must abide by its laws. Romans 13:1 clearly says, "Let every person be subject to the governing authorities. For there is no authority except from God, and those that exist have been instituted by God." My fleshly desire yearned to harbor Suzelynda, but I knew if Michael and I did this we would be handing out our own idea of justice instead of trusting in the God who is justice.

With deep sorrow we came to her that next morning to tell her the news.

"Suze, we have something to tell you. Let's all go sit down in the living room," Michael said.

As she approached the sofa, I could tell by her stare she knew something was wrong. Her body was rigid and tense and the silence in the room was deafening.

"Sweetheart come sit close to me, not over there in the chair," I said.

Putting my arm around her shoulder and hugging her, I softly said in a quivering voice, "Your work permit with the Newbolds was denied."

We began to weep together at the sad news.

Michael came and encircled us both and said, "Let's pray."

I don't remember what he said but afterwards we sat there for a long time paralyzed by this tragic news. None of us knew what to do but I knew I must seek the Lord and trust Him now more than ever.

God answered our prayers quickly that day as a plan was beginning to take shape for Suze. At the time of the news, the ministry had a wonderful mission team from Georgia serving with us over Christmas break. Fortunately, one of the participants was an American woman married to a Haitian man. She and Suze had hit it off from the get-go speaking back and forth fluently in Creole. Amazingly over four short days they had already formed a great friendship and were in the process of planning a trip to Haiti together soon.

At the same time, over the course of the past year, Suzelynda had been telling us she hoped to someday go back to her native land and minister to her people, to teach others about Jesus and what it meant to follow Him. God had clearly planted that desire and was now seeing it into fruition. "Delight yourself in the Lord, and He will give you the desires of your heart," from Psalm 37:4 came to mind as I thought about what was coming to pass in Suze's life.

Once we told this American woman, Noelle, of Suzelynda's situation she immediately arranged for Suze to go live with her husband's family in Haiti. Many of our team members did not understand why Suzelynda could not go to Haiti and live with her own family but each time I shared this news with other mission participants, I had to explain the situation.

"Yes, Suze was born in Haiti, but she traveled to the Bahamas when she was in elementary school," I told the mission team at dinner. "Although her family is here in our town her Dad disowned her and does not want anything to do with her," I went on to say.

"By disowning Suzelynda, she was prohibited to contact her family in Haiti, too. Since this was the situation, she did not have anyone to live with in her home country, either. The rejection by both the government and her biological family seemed cruel. *How could a country do this?* When she arrived in the Bahamas at age nine, Suze had been immersed in the Bahamian culture and learned English. She attended school and had grown up living like a Bahamian, yet now she could not attain residency or even a work permit.

This problem was common for most of the Haitians. Whether they had migrated at a young age or had been born in the Bahamas, they still had to apply for a permit to live there legally. Stateless, Haitians had to wait until they turned eighteen but once they reached that age, a Haitian applicant was faced with navigating a challenging and costly process. Most Haitians could not afford to go through the system and even if they could, they usually were denied. Jobs were limited in the Bahamas there-fore most Haitians were unable to remain with family and community once they were rejected. The situation is heart wrenching for most and leads to many families being separated. Yet the law was the law and we explained to our family and especially Suze that God is sovereign over the law.

One night at dinner we explained to our kids, "God appoints those in the law and if we believe in Jesus, we must believe in His ability to change or adjust the law as well," Michael said.

"But Mom, it seems so unfair. Why would God do this?" Josie asked.

"Well, guys, God always knows best, He has our entire lives in the palms of His hand. He knows the whole plan for each of our lives, whereas we only see a little at a time. We must trust Him; God's way will always be the best way," I said.

Michael added, "In this case, kids, He must be using the law to answer Suze's prayers and send her back to Haiti. He is taking her to the Haitian people where she can tell what she has learned about Jesus and share it with others." God, because of who He is, and because of Noelle's kindness, has provided a place for Suze to live in Haiti."

We quickly got all the details of this plan worked out and in two days a whole new life was about to begin for Suzelynda. The next morning, we boarded the boat to travel to the Nassau airport where she would fly to Haiti. I was soaking in every detail of our time together. Once we arrived in Nassau, we treated ourselves to the last meal we would share for months to come. We relished our conversation reliving the fun times in years past and ended our celebration collapsing into bed that night. Exhausted from the emotional roller coaster we had been on leading up to this moment, we knelt side by side to pray together, lifting our hearts to God through our tears. We ended our time worshipping God for his goodness.

There were more tears to come in our painful goodbye that next morning as we entered the airport. *Oh Lord please provide for Suze as she starts this new page in your book of life. You know the plans you have for her Lord, plans to prosper her and not to harm her, plans to give her hope and a future.* My silent thoughts rose to the Heavens as I watched Suze's small plane rise into the distant sky.

As the days turned into weeks, I pleaded with God to allow me to visit Suze. *Lord, I am not anxious about this situation, but instead am grateful for the gift of her in my life. I am submitting to you and thanking you. Only you could have given her the desire to go back to Haiti and the ability to do so. But, Lord, I want so much to see her again. Please make a way, I pray. In Jesus Name, I ask. Amen.*

* * * * * * *

2015 began in earnest as many teams returned and others came for the first time. While we worked alongside each one, Suzelynda was constantly on my mind. I continued to press in and ask God to be able to see her and patiently waited for the Lord to answer. Focusing on intentional discipleship among the teen girls in Blackwood replaced my longings for Suze. Since most of the Blackwood youth had professed belief in the gospel, we continued to teach biblical truth but also encouraged and equipped the older teens to become leaders in the church community themselves.

Thankfully, building the actual church building kept us very busy as well. As teams came on mission, they would each contribute to a different phase of the project. Placing my attention on these many areas of ministry kept me from focusing on the disappointment of Suzelynda's absence. In the middle of April, I finally heard the Holy Spirit's response, *Yes, go Amy; go as soon as you can.*

I was elated with this clear answer from the Holy Spirit.

The question was, would Michael be elated as well? I would soon find out.

Chapter 21

Trust and Obey for
There's No Other Way

*The Spirit of the LORD God is upon me, because the
LORD has anointed me to bring good news to the poor;
he has sent me to bind up the brokenhearted, to proclaim
liberty to the captives, and the opening of the prison to
those who are bound;...*

Isaiah 61:1

I quickly found out Michael's attitude about me taking a trip to Haiti. As I joyfully relayed to him that the Holy Spirit had told me it was the right time to go to Haiti and check on Suze, he not only disagreed but was strongly opposed when I mentioned my epiphany.

"You CANNOT go to Haiti by yourself, Amy!"

I said nothing but calmly replied, "But God told me to go-and as soon as possible." I trusted God and kept silent.

Several days went by. I was diligent to pray every morning, begging the Holy Spirit to change Michael's heart. I knew if God really had spoken to me, we had to have unity and peace about it. Otherwise, I was mistaken about what I heard. Scripture from Matthew 18:19 reminded me, "Again I say to you, if two of you agree on earth about anything they ask, it will be done for them by my Father in heaven."

Finally, almost a week later, God changed Michael's heart. *It had been the Holy Spirit, I knew it,* I thought. Michael agreed I should go and soon. I booked a ticket for two weeks away to see Suze. In a very short time we would be reunited! God had told me she was lost and needed direction. Phone communication was challenging and in the few lengthy conversations I had wept with her over the static of the connection. I knew it would help if I was there in person. I reflected on the circumstances leading up to Michael's "yes."

Suze was essentially living in a foreign country; it did not matter that the people around her were the same nationality. She did not know how to convert the two money systems, how to open a bank account, how to navigate a whole new way of life. Even school had become difficult since in Haiti they teach in French not Creole. She knew some French because the spoken language was similar, but she did not know how to write it at all.

Michael and I had decided to hire a private tutor for her after the headmaster of a private missionary-led school, Mr. Smith, had e-mailed us saying it would be best for her to re-take most of high school, so she could graduate. He let us know it was too complicated for her to learn in French until she knew how to speak and write the language. All this news was disheartening.

Even more discouragement came when I learned the woman Suzelynda was living with only had a one-bedroom apartment where they shared a double bed at night. This home also did not have a refrigerator or any type of kitchen but instead she and Suze cooked outside on a fire. Further details about the apartment complex really had me concerned when I learned twenty-two people shared only one bathroom.

I sought God for guidance and reached out to friends to pray for me and Suzelynda too. One day shortly before I was to leave for Haiti my friend Heidi told me about a ministry in Gressier.

"Amy, have you heard of the book about Voodoo Mountain?" She asked.

"No, what is it about?"

"It's a story of an American girl who has a ministry in Haiti only 25 minutes away from where Suze lives now. God told me to tell you about the book and the work there. Maybe Suze could find a position serving with them," Heidi said.

After the recommendation came from Mr. Smith to re-take up to three years of high school, Suze, Michael and I prayed about what to do. My trip to see her would provide God's answer. Suze felt like God wanted her to work in ministry and so we were going to stand on God's Word in John 10:9, "I am the door." Michael and I concluded at the end of our prayer time that if Jesus is the door and He wants Suze to work for Him, he will lead her to an opportunity. We believed God had a plan and would remove all obstacles, replacing our impossible with His possible if it was indeed His will. We had to rest in faith and watch Him act. I knew God was sending me to encourage Suze to watch God unfold His way in Haiti.

* * * * * * *

As I boarded my plane late in April of 2015, I felt an almost tangible peace and joy. I was beside myself to be able to go to be with Suze and experience the country of our beloved Haitian friends and family. It had been a deep desire of mine to go there and better understand the language and the culture of the people we ministered to. I longed to see where they came from and why they left, as it would help me better understand my sweet adopted sojourners.

When we flew in sight of the island, I saw a myriad of shanty houses cascading up the mountains, but the poverty did not dishearten me. What surprised me was the sight of the immense mountains. I knew about the topography of Haiti, but to fly in next to these enormous peaks took my breath away; they were staggeringly beautiful. For years, the images of the aftermath of the 2010 Haiti earthquake with its crumbling towns and widespread destruction had shaped my ideas of what I would see. Images of a war-torn, ugly country ran through my head.

When we landed in Port Au Prince remnants of the earthquake's destruction still remained, yet the natural beauty everywhere was overwhelming. I knew Haiti was God's home, for only our Creator could design such beauty. Scripture from Nahum 1:15 summarized how I felt, "Behold, upon the mountains, the feet of him who brings good news, who publishes peace!" Jesus clearly was here, and I had peace.

Regardless of this peace, there was a reality of navigating the airport, since my Creole was still not very good. I was cautious. In the Bahamas everyone spoke English, even the Haitian kids because it was a requirement at school; only at home did they speak Creole to their parents. However, even though most of them could speak the language, few could write it. In our Bible club times in Blackwood when I elicited help to learn Creole from the kids, I would run inevitably into road blocks when they couldn't write something out for me.

Suddenly, with people chattering in Creole all around me, I was over-joyed to hear Suze cry out, "Mom!"

She rounded the corner of the baggage claim area and I ran up to her. We held on tight to one another and cried for several minutes. *Finally, God... thank you Jezi!* Many people around us began clapping and cheering and I thought inwardly, *this is the angels in heaven rejoicing over us Jesus!* Thank you! Eventually we let go of one another and went to her friend's car to begin our journey to her home.

An hour and half later we arrived in Leogane, the town where Suze lived. Not knowing what our week would hold, we immediately sought God's direction for a job in full-time ministry job for her. Day after day we searched and prayed and had our own little mission trip visiting people in the hospital and on the streets talking about Jesus. We worshipped Jesus in everything we did fully enjoying our time together.

Prior to my trip I had e-mailed several mutual friends in various ministries located in Haiti and had been told about others that I was exploring for Suze. I promptly heard back from one on the nearby voodoo mountain that my friend had mentioned, a ministry called *Haiti Helps*. The e-mail explained we could visit and tour *Haiti Helps* on the days and times they have scheduled. For that week, the day would be Thursday. *Yikes,* I thought to myself. *I leave the following morning. Oh God please make this work,* I pleaded. Remembering to be thankful for any opportunity at this point, I went on to say, *Lord, you are in control; I trust you and thank you. Please allow this ministry to provide Suze with a job if it is your will for her.* By now, all other doors were being shut except this one at *Haiti Helps*.

The night before we were to visit, I wasn't so sure.

"Suze, I think this voodoo mountain ministry isn't really what I had in mind because it's thirty minutes away. But let's continue to be grateful and pray for direction. Resting with our mustard seed of faith, we can trust God to do the Impossible, right?"

"Absolutely, Mom," she said with conviction.

The plan was to arrive at *Haiti Helps,* eat at the ministry's cafe and then wait for our tour guide who would escort us up the mountain where the work was located.

From the beginning it seemed the enemy was in full force trying to derail our plan. *Ah, a good sign,* I thought. Turns out as we arrived to pick up the car, we rented for our 30-minute drive, we learned it was suddenly unavailable. Although we faced an invisible battle launched by the enemy, Suze and I were not about to give up.

"Who has a car we can borrow? Or better yet I can pay to borrow for the day, Suze?" I asked.

I recognized Satan's ploys since they were similar to those at the onset of constructing the church back in Blackwood. I quickly knew Suze and I needed to pray scripture. Using God's word- the sword of the Spirit-we prayed scripture from Isaiah 54:17 saying, "No weapon that is formed against you will prosper;" and also Genesis 50:20 which says, "As for you, you meant evil against me, but God meant it for good, ..." A sense of urgency was upon us as we repeatedly prayed God's word. *This is it,*

I thought. Why would Satan be trying so hard to stop us if Suze is not getting a job with this ministry?

Suddenly a car was found. Our driver Roodley speedily drove us to our lunch appointment. Amazingly, we arrived right on time, down to the minute. After a quick lunch we headed up the mountain to the location of the ministry.

On the tour of the facilities we met many lovely staff members and received wonderful insight into their work. But after almost 4 hours nothing had been said about a possible position there for Suze. I was looking for the Lord to naturally present a way for her to apply for a job with the ministry, but the tour seemed much more informative and my hope dwindled. *Oh no*, I prayed, *Lord all of this and nothing?* Just as my thoughts were culminating in doubt, Holly, the founder of the ministry, appeared. I knew she held our answer. After a short conversation she learned about Suzelynda and her need of a job. Holly gave us her business card and told us to please e-mail her about the possibility of employment.

That night after we were reviewing our day, Suze and I prayed and typed out an e-mail to Holly. Seeing God move miraculously to provide this opportunity instilled in us confidence and hope for the response. God had thrown our mountain of disbelief into the sea and shown us how amazing it is to live by faith.

This was on a Thursday. By the following Monday, Suze started another new chapter in her book of life at *Haiti Helps* Ministry.

I was able to travel home relieved knowing God had worked it out in getting a job for Suzelynda. Although we did not have firm confirmation at the time I left, the Holy Spirit's peace gave me assurance Suze would get the job.

On Monday morning, she messaged me and told me she was hired as a translator and was given the opportunity to move in with other Haitian girls who came from a similar abusive background. As God would have it, the name of the house where she was living was "Freedom House." God sent her from an island called "Freedom" to a new house called "Freedom," showing us He was truly in control! I was incredibly grateful for the time we had together and God's success. We had worshipped and prayed together, bonded by our love for one another. We had witnessed the power of defeating Satan's tactics using the word of God by calling "into existence the things that do not exist," as Romans 4:17 says.

Our faith had grown exponentially, and God's glory was revealed. Seeking Him gave both Suze and I more intimacy with Him as we had felt His abiding presence throughout our journey.

The Holy Spirit was so tangible on this trip I was certain He was now linking us to something new. Once I returned home, I told Michael all that had occurred, and we began to pray about what opportunities would be forthcoming. Since we loved Haitian people, we thought maybe the Lord would be moving us to Haiti. Confident He would show us, we stayed alert to Him. I also shared my heart and thoughts with our amazing Blackwood kids and as I was doing so these words just flowed out from the Holy Spirit one day as I was teaching at the Pavilion, "How many of you would like to go back to your home country and share the gospel with your Haitian brothers and sisters?"

Excitedly hands flew up into the air and many a "Yes!" was shouted. God planted the seed right there and then. As I relayed Suzelynda's journey to our Blackwood teens and young adults, I saw her story gave them comfort and hope.

A few short weeks after she had begun her new translator job, Suze called to tell me what was happening when she told the girls her age and her testimony.

"Mom, none of the girls can believe I did not try to figure out another way to stay in the Bahamas even though my first permit application was denied."

"Why?"

"Well, they think I am crazy to have left a nice life and family. But I told them how even when I was scared to move to Haiti, I had to because the government said so. I told them it was always God's plan to get me back my homeland, so I could minister to others what I was taught about God in the Bahamas."

"Some of the time I tell the girls about my Pa and what happened, too, and that makes them open up to me more. But I always tell them my heavenly Father is the One who took care of me through it all and that the only way I can know Him is because I have a relationship with Jesus. Usually that is when I tell them about Jesus, hoping they will want to have a friendship with him too."

"That is so wonderful Suze, so amazing. I am so very proud of you," I said lovingly choking back tears.

"You know, God's Word says in Revelation 12:11, "And they overcame him (Satan) because of the blood of the Lamb and because of the word of their testimony,..."

"What does that mean, Mom?"

"It means you are taking the enemy's ground in Haiti and replacing it with God's kingdom when you share your story. You also are evangelizing. You, sweetheart, are doing exactly what Jesus asks us all to do as followers of Him. I really can't tell you how thankful I am for your precious, amazing heart Suze! Oh, how we are so blessed."

Hanging up the phone, I rejoiced in telling Michael about how very good God was.

"Honey, can you believe Suzelynda's attitude?"

"Yes, I can. She spent years watching, learning and growing with us." He wasn't surprised at all.

"Using our difficult situations or our brokenness for God's glory is exactly what Jesus asks of us continually. Isn't that what we told her?" he added.

"Yes, but to see her joy just shows the transformation Jesus has done. I can't tell you how inspiring it is for me; that her faith is so real, and she is living it."

Conversations like this were repeated with anyone I thought would be willing to listen. Suze's boldness and trust gave our beloved Haitian teens motivation to follow Jesus and the desire to go on mission.

However, I was quickly faced with more challenges meant to derail my abundant joy. God made it plain to me and Michael that our mission was still incomplete. The church was almost finished in Blackwood but that was the point, "almost" is not "complete!" Our mission was becoming more urgent in our beloved Blackwood; we were to finish the church God had commanded us to build for His Haitian people.

As we strained toward finishing the construction, Satan's attempts to derail God's plan continued to come. Although His schemes were unknown, I was vigilant about praising God, reciting God's promises and claiming Jesus' blood and his name to pronounce victory.

Although I prayed continuously, I wondered if my confidence in Scripture would be enough.

Chapter 22

He's still Good and He's Still God!

My grace is sufficient for you, for my power is made perfect in weakness.

2 Corinthians 12:9

Amy, what are you typing?" Michael asked.

"Healing scriptures. Actually, all the ones we have been saying over Luke when the seizures come," I responded. I felt a little agitated by his question.

It was clear from the tense conversation that we were under stress. After returning from Haiti, my elation had quickly subsided when our son Luke became suddenly sick. What had begun with a phone call to pick him up from Camp quickly turned into a very serious situation. He was having massive seizures that left him gasping for air while violently shaking and rocking side to side. After the first seizure, rumors circulated quickly that voodoo had been placed on him. Luke in turn had become fearful.

"You really think Luke can say those verses while he is having an attack, Amy?" Michael snapped back.

"No, Michael, these are for us and for Luke only when He can say them. That would mean when he is not having a seizure. They are for our family. We have to stay united."

We used our best armor, God's Word, to defend Luke when the attacks came, just as we had done all year and just as I had in Haiti. God alerted me through the Holy Spirit that the unseen enemy was coming and even stronger than ever. Now I understood why He had cautioned me. If Satan could cause chaos and confusion in our family through an illness, he could take our attention away from building God's ministry and more importantly completing His church.

During this time of family storm, we had to keep our eyes fixed on Jesus or we would drown. I was clinging to scripture like Hebrews 12:2 paraphrasing it, saying the words for encouragement throughout my day. "Keep your eyes on Jesus, Amy, He both began and finished this race. He could put up with anything along the way; cross, shame or whatever. So, can you. With Jesus' help."

Equipping me and my family to face this challenge with Luke became a top priority. Medically speaking, no one could give us an answer for his strange seizures. As the summer teams concluded and we headed into fall, we knew we needed to persevere and dig in. Satan was not going to have victory. Prayers were solicited from everyone we knew in ministry, and our local Pastor, his wife, a church elder and friends came to our home to pray over Luke. Even though we were doing as much as we could with God's direction, the seizures grew worse. Luke's blood pressure dropped dangerously low and some of the episodes would last for several hours.

Faith, I knew we must have faith. Finally, by mid-September after an unsuccessful trip to see a specialist in Nassau, we decided we had to fly to the US to seek further help. Nothing was changing, and Luke was getting worse.

Living on a small island also caused me angst because we were so far away from proper medical care.

I pleaded with Michael, "What happens if he stops breathing? We live on a tiny island and flying anywhere quickly could be dangerous for him," I implored.

"Ok, Amy, I totally agree, we have to go to the US."

We planned a trip to Ft. Lauderdale in Florida to St. Joe DiMaggio's Children's Hospital. We heard from the local Bahamians that it had a good reputation.

After a quick journey to Florida and admission to the hospital, we quickly found out the US doctors were dismayed as well.

"Mr. and Mrs. Boykin, we don't know what's causing this," they said.

"How old did you say he was again?"

"Um, he just turned thirteen," I responded, wondering why they would ask.

"Well, all the tests come back negative. The CAT scan, MRI, everything. Are you certain he is not taking drugs? I think our only option is to administer a drug test now; do we have your permission to do so?"

We all were stunned by their question and sat there in silence for a moment.

"Of course not, he absolutely is not on drugs!" I was at my breaking point and offended this Doctor would suggest such a thing.

He went on looking at Michael, Luke and I, his finger pointing to the assessment.

"The nurse will bring in the forms for you to sign so we can draw more blood, or we can issue discharge papers. Those are your only options."

"Can't you see? If he were on drugs, we would not have flown all the way here from the Bahamas, desperate for answers. I would have taken him straight to a rehabilitation facility!" My emotions were clearly showing.

"Amy, settle down, they are just doing their job," Michael said. "Yes, doctor, we are fine with you taking more blood, but we know the tests will be negative." Michael patted my arm as he spoke.

It was a ridiculous question, but it immediately alerted me to the fact that the secular world would not be able to give me an answer for the unexplainable. We knew strange illnesses were not usually of the Lord but an attack of spiritual forces. We had even witnessed a man dying because of supposed voodoo placed on him back at home. Now, with this absurd question about my son being on drugs and no answers given by professionals, I knew the Lord was teaching me He was my hope and physician. I knew one of His names is Jehovah Rapha, "The Lord Who Heals." Clearly my fear had taken away my confidence in God's ability to restore Luke's health. I had forgotten He alone would provide the way for Luke's healing. I also knew we had to press in and ask God what to do.

After this epiphany, it did not surprise me that the many doctors could not give us a diagnosis. Looking at the total picture I asked God for His wisdom, encouraged by James 1:5, "If any of you lacks wisdom, let him ask God, who gives generously to all without reproach, and it will be given to him."

Searching intently in scripture for answers, the Holy Spirit enlightened me to look at Nehemiah's leadership again, just as He had done at the onset of the construction of the church building.

Studying his story for clues, I saw when he learned the wall in God's chosen city of Jerusalem lay in ruins, he was immediately grief stricken and sought the Lord in prayer. Nehemiah realized this physical boundary directly correlated to the spiritual boundary of the Jewish people. Both the city and the people's hearts lay in ruin.

Looking at his opening prayer, I immediately saw how Nehemiah included himself and his family in the confession of sins. Nehemiah 1:6 says, "…let the ear be attentive and your eyes open, to hear the prayer of your servant that I now pray before you day and night for the people of Israel are your servants, confessing the sins of the people of Israel, which we have sinned against you. Even I and my father's house have sinned…."

Seeing the words "we" and "Even I and my father's house" meant Nehemiah was including himself in the sin of the Israelite people. Although he had not met the Israelites he was referring to, and to my knowledge was not referring to a specific sin he or his family were repenting from, he knew the power of sin and forgiveness.

This passage showed me that whether our family had sinned, or this was ancestral sin, it did not matter, we must humbly repent of both. The physical wall of our family was breached; already we were playing into the enemy's hand through our disunity. I got it now, our hearts and physical boundaries had to be repaired.

I knew we also must not harbor any judgement or ill will towards one another or anyone because if we did, the result could be bitterness, condemnation or resentment springing up within our hearts.

Nehemiah's prayer would become the model for me and my family. Using it as our template, we confessed corporate sin as a family and individual sin and asked for God's mercy and grace to change us and allow us to forgive one another and anyone else. The passage in Nehemiah 1:11, "O Lord, let your ear be attentive to the prayer of your servant, and to the prayer of your servants who delight to fear your name, and give success to your servant today, and grant him mercy in the sight of this man," gave us hope as we saw God was a God of grace. Fear was one of the enemy's chief tactics in disrupting our unity. As we continued to press in, reciting God's word and claiming victory by Jesus' blood, we quickly discovered the free gift of Jesus' amazing grace.

Because of God's grace alone we would find Luke healed, in spite of our natural world telling us there were no answers. Confident in who we are because of Jesus, we returned from the US hopeful despite unanswered questions and no diagnosis.

Before returning to the US, we immediately jumped in to serving with a mission team from Alabama and met a participant, Barbara, who witnessed Luke's seizure. The next day Barbara came to me privately and said she thought it was a heart problem as she had a similar condition in her own life. Barbara referred us to her doctor in Birmingham who dealt with cardiology issues. She gave us a way in to see her as she normally did not see minors and was booked six months out for an appointment. Now in only two short weeks we would return to the US for this upcoming appointment.

We left in mid-October, flying to Florida then driving from Ft. Lauderdale to Birmingham. After a two-day drive, we arrived exhausted but hopeful. We immediately saw God's grace at work as the physician, a Dr. Valdez, diagnosed Luke within an hour of his examination. The seizures were a condition called POTS, Postural Orthostatic Tachycardia Syndrome. We found out this new syndrome was greatly misunderstood and there was very little research on it within the medical community. It is basically a form of dysautonomia that affects the flow of blood throughout the body. Luke's seizures were a result of the heart not pumping enough blood to the brain. Luckily, the treatment was simple: with proper medication, diet and a new health regime, Luke's seizures would eventually be under control.

We celebrated this new revelation and thanked Dr. Valdez. We were very grateful for her revelation of the condition that would set Luke free from Satan's attacks and were overcome by the next blessing we received.

During the examination she had asked Luke, "What do you do when these seizures come on?"

Startled by the question Luke responded, "Well, I pray."

I saw her eyes begin to tear up and knew she was a Christian as she said, "Well that is the best thing any of us could ever do, Luke."

We thanked Dr. Valdez and left the examination room giving God all the glory for connecting us and sending us these answers. When we checked out at the front desk, the nurse told us Dr. Valdez had instructed them to refund the full one-thousand-dollar amount of the office visit. She knew we did not have American health insurance and that we were missionaries. An even further favor occurred weeks later after one of our relatives generously paid for all of Luke's other hospital bills, plus our travel expenses.

What would have taken our family years to pay off now was wiped out overnight.

Clearly, seeking God's wisdom, using His word in prayer and claiming His promises had allowed Him to lead us to the right answers, conquer the forces of darkness and gave us more assurance of Jesus' nature. We triumphed in the situation knowing firsthand the reality of Jesus' grace. It made sense that the hospitals had no idea what was going on as well, since the condition Luke finally was diagnosed with affects .01% of the population and is only been studied and diagnosed within the past thirty years. This knowledge was more confirmation of God's triumph!

****

Returning home to the Bahamas, I got back into my regular morning prayer time, and asked God what was next. His directive was to continue building. It was obvious this was from God because only He could give a directive like this after our family had learnt and used Nehemiah's story as part of our armor. As I prayed for enlightenment, I felt the Holy Spirit telling me, *build your family's protective wall like Nehemiah did, but also continue to build the church.*

God's reminder revealed that when we had stopped focusing our attention on the church building and instead focused on Luke and ourselves, donations to complete the church building project had come to a halt. The physical building had been completed by September, but we needed furnishings and leadership. Up until this point we had been using our picnic tables for the Bible club, discipleship groups and weekly service and although they sufficed, adequate seating and electronics such as a TV screen and sound system would help make the church official. Even more crucial was God's answer to who would become the church's elders, deacons, and Pastor. While we waited for finances, we could not turn over the church to the local people. We knew we must pray and re-focus.

God revealed we should e-mail a request for funds to the ministry supporters. Financial relief for the building came immediately from a generous anonymous donor which resulted in getting the electronics and furnishings to complete the interiors of the building. By the end of November, we experienced amazing victory in our family, with a solution to Luke's illness and in provision for the church building.

THE WAY

We will never know until eternity if Luke's attack was what Paul de-scribes as "a thorn in the flesh" given to Luke to perfect God's power in His weakness or whether it was to teach our family to take every thought captive to the obedience of Christ. Regardless of God's reason for Luke's seizures, my family and I learned that the only way to break strongholds was by appropriating God's word in our life.

Another critical lesson our family also learned was there is an invisible war being waged between light and darkness, one not to be taken lightly. Defending ourselves just as Nehemiah did by saying scripture such as Nehemiah 4:14, "Do not be afraid of them. Remember the Lord, who is great and awesome, and fight for your brothers, your sons, your daugh-ters, your wives, and your homes," guarded us and defeated evil.

Although the entire experience of Luke's sickness was painstaking to endure as a parent and as a family, God ultimately used this situation for His glory as He revealed His goodness. What we as a family realized was that God used this trial and the others to knit us together to him and to one another. The entire experience took our focus away from ourselves and shifted our gaze solely on Jesus.

As it says in 1 Peter 5:10, "And after a little while, the God of all grace, who has called you to his eternal glory in Christ, will himself restore, confirm, strengthen, and establish you." Our family and ministry knew this and had lived it. We rejoiced in knowing God's plan is the best and always for our benefit if we will only believe and trust in His Way. The entire situation showed God's amazing character which is good and glorious and filled with grace.

* * * * * * *

Soon after our return we prepared for our first ever Thanksgiving service with the ministry successfully feeding over two hundred Haitian people in the community. Thanksgiving spilled into Christmas and we had our best Christmas celebration ever in Blackwood with our own local Bahamian church, The People's Church. We also participated in Christmas gift spon-sorship together with an Alabama church which had faithfully supported God's ministry with us since the beginning. God was continuing to bless His people, bear His fruit and make His name known to many.

With the church almost complete in 2015 we made a final push to fast and pray for leadership in Blackwood. God told us our mission was to complete the church and empower the local Haitian people with the gospel, so they could teach and preach to their own people. Armed with determination now, our stronger faith gave us a renewed sense of purpose as Isaiah 40:31 says, "…but they who wait for the LORD shall renew their strength; they shall mount up with wings like eagles; they shall run and not be weary; they shall walk and not faint."

If the enemy thought he could harm us by causing dissension within our family, he was gravely mistaken. In fact, it was quite the opposite as we knew God's sovereignty had reigned. God used Luke's illness in our lives to reveal the magnitude of His grace. Seeing only the Gospel could cleanse and purify us from any predicament drew me personally into a deeper, abiding relationship with the Lord. The transformational power of God's grace now gave us momentum to listen for Christ's ultimate plan for His church. Patiently we would wait until He answered our requests taking one step at a time, glorifying God in all that He was doing.

Chapter 23

New Year, Same Jesus

*And there is salvation in no one else, for there is
no other name under the heaven given among men
by which we must be saved.*

Acts 4:12

This newfound grace our family had experienced in the Fall of 2015 spilled over by blessing the ministry with a continuation of God's fruit. For years we had plugged away teaching, preaching, equipping and evangelizing the young people and yet there were still a few older Haitian teens who had not made a profession of faith. We were keenly aware that the Holy Spirit changes hearts, so we stayed grounded in this truth and true to our mandate which was to love our neighbors and teach them the gospel. Pressing on, we received the best gift from the Lord on New Year's Day of 2016.

The phone rang early in the morning. I stumbled to answer it, so I would not wake Michael. It was Roseline, one of the girls in Blackwood.

"Ms. Amy, I need to talk to you; actually, see you," she said.

"What's up Roseline? Are you ok?" I said, concern in my voice.

Quietly leaving my bed and going into the bathroom I shut my door and said, "You sound worried."

"No, no, Ms. Amy, it's just that, um, well, I need to talk to you in person. Can I come over on the ferry to your house now?" she asked.

"Now? Like right now? What time is it?"

"I don't know, I could come on the 7am ferry. I think that's in thirty minutes or so," she replied somewhat anxiously.

"Ok, sweetheart, I will be at the dock to pick you up."

Hanging up, I thought to myself, *Oh no, what could this be?* I knew Roseline very well. She was an older teen who had been coming to all the ministry functions for two years. She was very smart and a natural leader. I knew a lot of intimate details about her own past abuse by her Father and the estrangement that had occurred within her family because of her allegations against him. She had shared her life and her family's life with me in full confidence. We regularly spent time with she and her older brother Robensen, her mother Jenniflore and youngest sister Carline.

Sometimes the family needed money for food and we gladly gave it. Other times they needed a simple hug or the opportunity to work; we supplied that, too. God had given us such a privilege to share with others, we readily obliged so we could show His love and teach others about Him. The only drawback was the family were members of the Jehovah's Witness. We had prayed for many years for their conversion, but God had not moved upon their hearts and minds; yet that is.

All of that was about to change.

As I picked Roseline up at the dock in Spanish Wells and hugged her, we wished one another a Happy New Year. She smiled at me, but I knew her well enough to know she was distraught. She looked nervous.

"Let's go to our special spot, the beach at the end of the island and talk. Does that sound like a good plan?" I said, trying to reassure her.

"Ok," she said, a smile creeping over her face.

Inwardly I had been praying hard since the phone call wondering what could be so pressing. *Was she pregnant,* I wondered? *Had something bad happened with her father?* I asked the Holy Spirit, but no answers were given. I felt God's peace, a clear sign things were probably okay.

The day was perfect. We parked my golf cart, so we could stare into the beautiful ocean. The January skies were crisp and clear, and the sun was just beginning to peek through the early morning clouds. God's beauty enveloped us as I encouraged her to tell me what was going on. As Roseline began she talked about how confused she had felt for many months about who she was as a person. She knew Jesus wanted her to become His and the battle within her had been difficult because she felt allegiance to her congregation at the Jehovah's Witness Fellowship.

She went on to explain that when she was abused by her Father, her Haitian Baptist Church had condemned her and her family. They told her how wrong she was for telling them about her Dad's abuse. This made her angry at God and she questioned the church. Instead, the Jehovah's Witness reached out to her family and gave them love and support. They financially provided, too, so her whole family moved from the church she had grown up in and joined the Jehovah's Witness congregation.

But Roseline knew they were not teaching the truth of the Bible. She had heard and seen who God really was by being around our family and the ministry. She concluded that she had to commit her life to Jesus.

With tears streaming down my face, I asked, "Have you told your Mom?"

"Yes, we talked about two days ago," she replied.

"Ok, just repeat this prayer after me then, Roseline. You can ask Jesus into your heart right now."

After we prayed, I hugged her, and we laughed and cried. Then she interrupted me, "Oh Ms. Amy, God told me I must get baptized; like today."

"Um, well we have the Christmas mission team here Roseline, I will have to see..."

"No, today, it has to happen, but I need my family to be there too. It is the first day of the new year and this is why I had to come so early. I knew God wanted me to begin my new chapter today. So pleeaasseee can you figure out when I can get baptized today?" she pleaded.

"Of course, and I promise it will happen today," I said confidently.

Later that afternoon we took our mission team down to the beach in Blackwood and baptized Roseline along with some mission team participants and a younger Haitian boy.

* * * * * * *

The blessing of God's work still growing was great confirmation and encouragement for me, Michael and our family. Thanking God, we continued to seek Him for what was next. A plan unfolded the following week after Michael's morning prayer time.

"Amy, God gave me the next thing we need to accomplish for His ministry," Michael said.

"Remember when you asked the Blackwood kids about going back to Haiti?"

"Yes."

"Well, I clearly heard God say that since we cannot legally take the Haitian kids to Haiti yet on a mission trip, we can take them to their own people on another island to evangelize."

"What?!" I responded in disbelief. We'd never talked about this idea before.

203

"Amy, we can take Frantz with us and he can chaperone the teens and mentor them like I do," Michael said excitedly.

Frantz was the young man who was good friends with both Jean and Davidson. We had employed him full time in the ministry, caring for the grounds of the church and assisting Michael in the day to day operations and with the youth. Frantz was learning and growing in God's word and although quiet in demeanor, he was faithful. He loved having responsibilities and thrived in learning God's word.

It was clear from Michael's voice this was God's plan. He went on saying, "If we teach the young adults, we have been discipling all these years what it looks like to live out belief in Christ we will be reaching more youth and spreading the gospel."

As I thought about it, the plan sounded right, putting together the puzzle pieces Michael suggested.

"Frantz would be a perfect choice for the trip since both Jean and Davidson had full time jobs," I said.

As Michael and I gave God praise for His revelation, we moved forward with His will to take some of the Haitian youth on their first mission trip.

We were also aware of a larger Haitian community on another Bahamian island and prayed about a plan from God as to how to go about this weekend. He said to meet their needs and preach the gospel. This looked like supplying people with bags of basic necessities such as toothpaste, toothbrushes and soap. We hoped this would provide us an introduction to talking and meeting people where we could share about Jesus and His plan of salvation. Since the ministry funds all the programs we had to first pray for money for this weekend trip and for the completion of the church. Gratefully, God responded with funds that were given to me personally by the passing of my own earthly father.

With the necessary finances in place I was able to quickly schedule and plan the youth mission trip to occur at the end of February. Michael and I also decided to take our entire family and provide the way for an American intern and Bahamian friend to serve with us. After thanking God for his outpouring of generosity it felt like we were living out the book of Acts in modern day times. This pattern of presenting the gospel to new people, along with experiencing rejection and persecutions, reminded me of Paul and what the early church endured as they spread the gospel.

James 1:2–4 says," Count it all joy, my brothers, when you meet trials of various kinds, for you know that the testing of your faith produces steadfastness. And let steadfastness have its full effect, that you may be perfect and complete, lacking in nothing."

I also knew that was the attitude I was to have, and I rejoiced to be counted worthy to be used to bring Jesus' name to other people no matter what the cost. As twenty-four of us embarked upon the weekend mission trip we had no idea what to expect. I prayed we would be able to endure whatever God sent our way with the same attitude Christ showed.

When we arrived at the Haitian community in Nassau it looked like Blackwood with shanty homes connected by small alley ways. Kids ran around shoddily dressed but their smiles and love engaged all our hearts. We reunited with some of our former Haitian residents and met many in need. We circled up and prayed and allowed our youth to go out into the community and distribute the bags of necessities as well as share the gospel. That trip bore wonderful fruit of intentional evangelization and opened the eyes of our Haitian youth.

"Mr. Michael, I had no idea there were people who had less than us," Gregory responded.

Gregory was an older teen who was very smart and growing in his walk with the Lord. He had been one of the first youth to profess faith in Jesus in the Summer of 2013 and he was a regular disciple of the ministry.

"I can't wait to say thank you to my Mom who works so hard to take care of me and my sister," he went on to say.

Although none of the Haitians we met on that trip made declarations for Jesus, our own Haitian youth learned a lot about how Jesus supplies their needs and about being grateful. Many had no idea there were those who were less fortunate than themselves. By the end of the trip most were powerfully affected by serving and we too were thankful to be able to show them what it looks like to live with the same mindset Jesus had. I was reminded of the Apostle Paul's words in Acts 20:35, "In all things I have shown you that by working hard in this way we must help the weak and remember the words of the Lord Jesus, how he himself said, "It is more blessed to give than to receive."

Other seeds were also planted during this trip. Whether the youth encountered the power of Jesus by ministering to the community or by simply participating in the journey, the impact was far reaching as it taught them the importance of being obedient to the gospel. As Matthew 16:24 says, "Then Jesus told his disciples, "If anyone would come after me, let him deny himself and take up his cross and follow me."

The teens now understood firsthand the impact of leaving their security in Blackwood for the unknown in Nassau. They learned that like Jesus whatever cross they had to bear would be for eternal glory. Their obedience could affect another person's eternity as well as strengthen their own faith. In the end, the trip was successful because God's name was proclaimed, and His glory furthered. Triumph was claimed because the youth encountered the power of living out the gospel and showing Christ's love.

As we left Nassau for the journey back to our island, we reveled in our mountain-top experience on that weekend mission trip. But inwardly I knew that with every mountain came a valley. As I prayed silently, I asked the Lord for courage to prevail and for the answers to our church leadership questions to come quickly.

Lord, I am unbelievably grateful, but I also know that our plan is not finished. Give us your church leadership, Lord, and give me the strength to remain courageous. And finally, let me, my family and the ministry put on the whole armor of God, Amen.

Chapter 24

Glorious Grace –
Living Counterintuitively

*But if it is by grace, it is no longer on the basis of works,
otherwise grace would no longer be grace.*

Hebrews 11:6

THE WAY

I greeted the ladies in Creole as they filed in for our women's Bible Study.

"Bonjou madams, koman ye?"

As I said good morning and hugged them, they each responded in English, "Good morning, Ms. Amy, how are you?"

The hugs were plentiful and many crowded around me saying, "Merci, merci, Ms. Amy!"

It was clear from the ladies' sweet embraces and many thank-yous that they were grateful for Michael and I taking their daughters and sons to Nassau. The mission trip had been a powerful time, not only for the teens but also for the community because it showed their mission was just like ours. Being a "missionary" was not a title for a few elect people. I constantly was telling our church community the word 'missionary' applied to all of us who believe and follow Jesus. Ultimately, loving Jesus would overflow into loving our neighbors naturally. Being a firm believer that actions speak louder than words, I constantly challenged everyone's mindsets about what living for Jesus looked like as an authentic believer. Today, most importantly, I was grateful God had given us the idea and means to further His kingdom and plant more seeds. I loved my Haitian family more than ever and was grateful to see their humility and joy.

Over the course of the past year, the Haitian women and I had been experiencing a beautiful mutual affection for one another. Meeting to discuss the Bible every Wednesday morning, we laughed at one another as we taught each other in our native languages. These women had become some of my closest friends and I treasured our time together.

This group of approximately twenty women had solidified in the Spring of 2015 after a mission team brought two ladies to serve with the ministry. These American Bible teachers led our first ever women's Bible study conference in Blackwood. The response was overwhelming and motivated me to continue teaching them the following year. I began by meeting weekly in the church building even though it was not complete. Over cookies and water, we prayed, laughed and cried as I read and taught the Bible outside or in the unfinished building.

Here we were a year later in the Spring of 2016 and I was leading a new study about grace. This was an unfamiliar idea and I knew it would be tough for the women to change mindsets. Most of the Bahamian and Haitian culture that were "churched" lived in strict adherence to the law in the Bible and not the Gospel. Sadly, this legalism permeated the thinking of the people, pastors and church members alike.

Many of them felt they could not come to church because of the unwritten, silent rule that they had to be good enough just to enter the building. Another false idea was that when a person did come to church, they must wear what we would call our "Sunday best." Some could afford nice clothes, but others would sacrifice to buy them in lieu of such basic needs as food. It was a desperate condition and stronghold the enemy had on the people of these nations that needed to be broken with the truth of the gospel of grace.

Although this would be a challenge, I also knew that "with God all things are possible."

That scripture from Matthew 19:26 was painted on our sign in the Pavilion in both Creole and English and was the foundational promise our ministry was founded upon. As God often does, the study on grace was perfectly suited for me and exactly what I needed to learn and hear as I taught the ladies.

"Ladies let's turn in our Bibles to Ephesians Chapter 2. We are going to be studying the subject of God's grace. I realize this is a concept some of us don't understand very well but God makes it very clear who we are because of His grace."

"Widelene, please begin at verse 1 through verse 10."

It was a long passage and she did her very best.

"And you were dead in the trespasses and sins in which you once walked, following the course of this world, following the prince of the power of the air, the spirit that is now at work in the sons of disobedience— among whom we all once lived in the passions of our flesh, carrying out the desires of the body and the mind, and were by nature children of wrath, like the rest of mankind. But God, being rich in mercy, because of the great love with which he loved us, even when we were dead in our trespasses, made us alive together with Christ by grace you have been saved and raised us up with him and seated us with him in the

heavenly places in Christ Jesus, so that in the coming ages he might show the immeasurable riches of his grace in kindness toward us in Christ Jesus. For by grace you have been saved through faith. And this is not your own doing; it is the gift of God, not a result of works, so that no one may boast. For we are his workmanship, created in Christ Jesus for good works, which God prepared beforehand, that we should walk in them."

As Widelene read in Creole I prayed to myself silently, *Oh Lord please help these ladies, this culture, understand who you are and who you are in us. Break the misunderstanding of working for your salvation and change their hearts, Holy Spirit. Give me the words and open their hearts to You-the truth-Jesus. In Your Name, Jesus. Amen.*

"Ok, I know there is a lot to take in right there. Let's open in prayer. Ms. Widelene, will you pray?"

After Widelene concluded, I looked at the ten or so ladies and asked, "Who can remember what "sin" is in the Bible? We talked about it last week."

Cassandra's hand shot up, "Ms. Amy, sin is when we don't wear our dresses and get our nails done before church. You know we get a lot of looks when that happen."

"Well, kind of Cassandra. Did you know this idea of having to dress a certain way is not in the Bible? The Bible says we come as we are to church. God cares about a person's heart not the hairstyle, the fancy shoes, or a long dress. But I realize a lot of you think you can only come if you have certain shoes and clothes."

I could tell from the look on their faces they clearly did not understand. I prayed, *Please Holy Spirit, Help!*

"Remember last week we spoke about sin meaning we missed the mark? One way the Bible teaches about sin is that we have been born with it and we go towards what we think of as evil instead of good. Last week we looked at several scriptures talking about when we were in our mother's womb, we had sin. It is a part of who we are from the get-go."

It seemed like they were understanding, so I went on.

"But God came and freely gave us a gift to cover our sins and that gift is Jesus. We know that from John 3:16. I know we all understand this verse well. Does anyone want to say it out loud now?"

Mirlande stood up quickly and recited the verse from memory, clearly proud of herself.

Now, let's look at Ephesians Chapter 2 again, specifically verse 8. Mirlande, since you volunteered please kindly read in Creole as I read it now in English, "For by grace you have been saved through faith. And this is not your own doing; it is the gift of God, not a result of works, so that no one may boast."

"What does this verse say about who saves us?"

"Ms. Amy can it be "grace?""

"Perfect Mirlande! Yes, and just before this key verse we learned that because God loves us so much, He allowed His son Jesus to die in place of our sins. This is "grace." Jesus' obedience to the Father's will is "grace" ladies!"

I then asked them what they thought the "gift" was in the verse.

Cassandra, who regularly also had ladies to her house for prayer meeting, said again, "Ms. Amy I think it's grace?"

"Yes, yes, good! Praise God you are understanding!"

"When we accepted Jesus, ladies, that meant we accepted what He did for us and that is called grace, it is a gift to us. Think of it like a gift someone brings you for your birthday but much, much better. We did not ask Jesus to die for our sins, but God chose that way so that we could have a relationship with Him. That friendship happens when we have Jesus in our hearts. And if Jesus is in each of us we have all that Jesus is inside of us too. We can now act like Jesus in every situation if we choose to think and act like Him!"

Before I could continue, Widelene said, "I have some questions. What does it mean when it says, "not a result of works so no one can boast, Ms. Amy?"

"Ah, exactly, that is my question to you ladies. Are you tired of trying to be good?"

I could tell by their quizzical looks no one understood.

"Do you believe if you come to church, prayer meeting, Bible study and do all of these "good" things you earn God's reward and He is happy with you?"

"Yes, yes!"

"No, it is good to do those things but not to earn your way to receive His love. You only receive His love by accepting the grace He offers each of us. You don't have to "do" anything. You have to rest in accepting Him and knowing who He is inside of you now."

"Let me give you an example. When someone does something that hurts us like gossips about us, we don't get mad or try to get even. We pray for them, we ask God to forgive them and we ask God to allow us to love them despite their words. The only way we can do this is when we cling to who Jesus is inside of us. He offers us forgiveness through grace and we must offer the same to others."

"What about our kids? I know you all help one another with your children and I know there are fights between children at your houses. Instead of re-acting in anger and hitting them with a wooden spoon, what if you stepped away and counted to ten, then asked yourself, "What would Jesus do now?" "Ladies, we must learn that we can respond and act like Jesus because He already took all our sin away when He died. When Jesus looks at us, He sees a holy, righteous person filled with himself. Having bad habits allows us to come to Him and ask Him to change us and make Him bigger than the bad habit. So instead of yelling, we walk away and ask Jesus to send His peace because He is peace. Since He is Peace, we have that peace in us, we need to choose it instead of yelling. Make sense?"

I went back to the first example, "Can someone tell me what you should do if some gossips about you?"

Blank stares were all I could see.

"Ok, what would be the opposite of gossip?"

Widelene said slowly, "Speak nice, Ms. Amy?"

"Yes, perfect Widelene!"

I had some suggestions of my own.

"We could pray for others and say nice words about them until later on, where your heart was not upset, and you could speak to them directly if you needed to do so."

"We can choose to act like Jesus instead of responding with bad habits we have been taught. That would be the way to show grace."

The life of legalism was engrained in this culture very deeply. I wanted to engage them in this re-training of their minds, so I thought of something interactive.

"Ok, let's divide into pairs. I want us to pretend the person in front of us has stolen clothes off our clothes line, or maybe your child hit the other person's child. I want you to look one another in the eye and say you forgive them and are sorry and that you love them even though they are the one who did the wrong. Then give the other person a hug."

The ladies turned their chairs to one another and hesitated. This was very unfamiliar territory for them, but they seemed to like the playacting and smiled when they finished.

"Ok, now, let's switch roles. The other lady must forgive now and show grace to the one who "did her wrong." Let's pretend this woman in front of you said mean, ugly things about you or your family. Maybe she even shared a private secret to the whole community that was only between you and her. I want you to look that lady in the eye and tell her you love her and forgive her. Then hug each other, and I mean a big one."

Something about the process touched me deeply as I reflected on my past year, and tears started welling up in my eyes Widelene saw and came over and put her arm around me, asking me in Creole, "What's wrong Ms. Amy?"

This kind gesture unleashed a flood of tears. I sobbed while she hugged me. One of the ladies began to sing *Amazing Grace* in Creole and the others joined in. These sweet women showed beautiful grace in the form of Jesus.

After they consoled me, I recounted through sniffles how the journey of the past 18 months had been difficult for me and my family. We continually wanted to pursue God's call and be faithful but with Luke's illness, sheer exhaustion, loneliness, and rejection I was spent. I knew God was teaching me I was a fellow pilgrim with my Haitian sisters and as such, teaching on grace was a perfect subject. I, too, would need to remember to cling to Jesus and allow His graceful presence to overwhelm me instead of succumbing to my feelings.

I was encouraging the ladies but cheering myself on, trying to convince myself to believe in God's very words. I knew if Jesus was in me, I had everything He is within me too; I had to choose grace and completely rely on Him. Full surrender was a continual process. Emptying myself magnified Jesus' overwhelming fullness and granted me a deeper abiding relationship with Him.

I was still feeling the weight of responsibility from managing so many mission teams. Plus, the demands of ministry, Luke's illness and persecution from people had caught up to me and I was exhausted. Clearly, I was doing things in my own strength and not relying on God's grace through Christ.

Ironically, this attitude of grace was the same lesson Jesus taught me at my initial surrender to His call. This life of grace was not a onetime event but a continual process of choosing to become like Jesus and love, forgive and serve. Putting on His gracious nature would show my complete love for Him and reveal that He indeed had the number one position in my heart. Living in grace was a lifestyle.

My small group study on grace coincided with Michael and I teaching the regularly scheduled church services every Sunday afternoon in Blackwood. Our sermon series also tied into grace as I thought about what it looks like to be unified in the body of Christ. For many Sundays we had been teaching what Paul taught the Corinthian church. In 1 Corinthians 1:10 Paul says, "I appeal to you, brothers, by the name of our Lord Jesus Christ, that all of you agree, and that there be no divisions among you, but that you be united in the same mind and the same judgement."

Paul goes on to illustrate what 'united' means in 1 Corinthians 12:12 when he says, "For just as the body is one and has many members, and all the members of the body, though many, are one body, so it is with Christ." He explains what this looks like by saying in verse 14, "For the body does not consist of one member but of many." Paraphrasing the rest of chapter 12, Paul then likens each one of us believers to a part of the body and concludes by saying that each part is needed and necessary, most especially the weakest part so "...that there may be no division in the body, but that the members may have the same care for one another. If one member suffers, all suffer together, if one member is honored, all rejoice together."

Finishing the ladies Bible Study with a closing prayer, I continued to rehash these details in my mind walking down the Blackwood trail to the dock. The Holy Spirit gave me an "aha" moment that I needed to choose His grace and pray for unity.

Seeking God, the next morning in my prayer time, I asked, *How should I rely on grace for unity, Lord??*

The Holy Spirit reminded me of 1 Corinthians 13 and highlighted verses 4–6, "Love is patient and kind; love does not envy or boast; it is not arrogant or rude. It does not insist on its own way; it is not irritable or resentful; it does not rejoice at wrongdoing but rejoices with the truth."

As I meditated on these scriptures, I understood from the Holy Spirit that turning inward and feeling sorry for myself about the way things were- disunified and legalistic- was not Christ-like. I knew from Philippians 1:29 it was a "gift" to suffer, "For it has been granted that for the sake of Christ you should not only believe in him but also suffer for his sake." The original meaning of the word "granted" meant "gift." I also realized that by Jesus' overcoming presence of His grace, I could choose to love like the 1 Corinthians 13 verses outlined. He had shown His successful plan time and time again. Digging in, forgoing my emotions, I trusted His grace.

Finally, after so many trials I decided to share my burdens with Michael.

"I am so, so tired, Michael. Will you pray for me?"

I felt an overwhelming sense of God's peace after his loving prayer and knew I was going to be okay.

I wanted to add something else.

"Can we also pray for God to direct us about the church leadership again, hon?"

Michael and I pleaded with God to reveal definitively His leadership for the Blackwood church. As we were fasting and praying one more time for the church completion, we heard nothing but silence. Then one morning as I knelt in prayer, God convicted me of my desperate need for repentance again. How I must choose His strength and grace and not lean on my own and be patient. "...for the joy of the Lord is your strength," from Nehemiah 8:10 came flooding through my mind.

God told me things would happen in His timing not our own. The answer of who was to shepherd the Haitian congregation would be revealed when God chose. By the end of my prayer time I had reached another turning point in my spiritual journey when I heard the Holy Spirit say, *Arise, Amy.*

After praying, I took courage in standing firm in Jesus again knowing He would show me in His perfect time just who His choice was to lead the church. The peace I had overwhelmed me and was a sure sign of God's presence and being in His will.

Chapter 25

The Journey of Endings
and New Beginnings

*And now I commend you to God and to the word of grace,
which is able to build you up and to give you the inheritance
among all those who are sanctified.*

Acts 20:32

My fervent prayers for leadership no longer consumed me as I embraced the day to day interaction of the ministry. I realized my pity party at the ladies Bible Study had taken me backwards, forgetting that praise always ushers in God's joy and defeats the enemy. Arming myself daily with thanksgiving scriptures and speaking the attributes of God helped me quickly focus on the upcoming teams for the Spring. In addition to the weekly activities that kept us busy, planning and preparing for the many mission teams that would soon be joining us became not only my focus but our ministry's direction as well. With students from two large colleges combining their Spring Breaks we needed to be ready to teach them about serving and loving like Jesus.

"What will we do with all these college kids arriving, Michael?" I was feeling anxious about the plans for our new arrivals.

"Well, like I told you before, God said our church is too small."

Michael had heard from the Lord as we were completing the church building the year before that we needed more room. When we were praying about the final construction, God told him to take another leap of faith and add on even before the building was finished. God already knew the space would be too small for the congregation that would be overflowing.

"Just like we see every week, we need more space for people to be gathering on Sundays," Michael replied.

"Yes, but how can we build another building? We don't have any funds in the ministry for that," I replied.

Although I'd seen God provide miraculously for His kingdom and for our family, my doubts still crept in. I knew the Holy Spirit was telling me to trust Him. The next morning, I cried out to Him in my prayer time, *Can I really trust You Lord?* He responded *Amy, give it all to Me.*

I sat still to listen and wait. I sensed the Holy Spirit was telling me to give the small remainder of the inheritance I had from my Dad. Instead, I tried to negotiate with God. *Finally, God my family and I have some financial relief beyond a few months. Are you sure you want me to use this money for the Discipleship building?*

I thought and prayed and debated for several more days in my prayer closet. *God why can't I use this for my children or better yet, a vacation for us that does not include ministry visits and getting ministry supplies?*

God was silent. However, as I looked at scripture in I Timothy I saw how God had changed my heart from the way it had been in my previous life in Texas. Chapter 6 verses 17–19 say, "As for the rich in this present age, charge them not to be haughty, nor to set their hopes on the uncertainty of riches, but on God, who richly provides us with everything to enjoy."

I paused and thought, *"What more could I enjoy than seeing my Haitian brothers and sisters have a place to worship God? Another building for more people to call home? What about future generations and families? Certainly, they would hear Jesus and lives would be changed, right God?*

As I read on, God answered from his Word. The passage ended saying, "They are to do good, to be rich in good works, to be generous and ready to share, thus storing up treasure for themselves as a good foundation for the future, so that they may take hold of that which is truly life." *Okay Lord, I want that which is "truly life,"* I whispered, tears forming in my eyes.

A few short weeks later we began the construction of the final building for the church. There were fifty-five mission team participants from two colleges serving with us on Spring Break. We knew we could quickly accomplish the task of erecting the eight hundred square foot structure that would become our Discipleship building.

We were half way towards finishing the foundation and framing when God spoke again to both Michael and me. He told us to seek financial support for the completion of the church and the interiors. We did not understand why He would ask us to do this since we had the funds to complete the building.

The next day as I was teaching our teams and Haitian youth about the importance of being a seed scatterer, I read from Mark 4:26, "And he (Jesus) said, "The kingdom of God is as if a man should scatter seed on the ground," the Holy Spirit spoke to me that this was a scripture for me and Michael. I explained the verse further to those who were listening and taught them that as followers we are called to speak God's Word (plant the seed) to everyone and thus it scatters.

THE WAY

Then a light bulb went off in my head. That's why God wanted us to ask for donors to the building project! Now I needed to go tell my husband.

"Michael, God wants others to be able to sow into His kingdom by donating so they too could receive the blessing of being a part of allowing others to use this building to speak and teach about Jesus."

"Um, let's look at those verses more later on tonight, Amy, since we're both busy now."

That night as we sat in bed, Michael and I looked at the scripture passage, seeking clarity. We were led to 2 Corinthians 9 verses 10 and 11, "He who supplies seed to the sower and bread for food will supply and multiply your seed for sowing and increase the harvest of your righteousness. You will be enriched in every way to be generous in every way, which through us will produce thanksgiving to God."

"Well, that makes sense," Michael said.

"Hon, God wants other people to be able to participate in furthering His eternal kingdom! This reveals the character of Jesus," I was thrilled with this revelation.

"Asking others to donate towards the Discipleship House will give them the blessing of building God's kingdom for Jesus' name. This is an eternal reward for the giver and receiver!" It was hard to contain my excitement.

"Sounds good, hon; I am on board. Let's send out an e-mail tomorrow; I don't want to slow down the construction process. Now turn out the lights, let's go to sleep!"

Next morning the first thing I did after my prayer time was send out an e-mail request to our core ministry supporters. We immediately got a response from the same generous donor who had given towards the completion of the church earlier in the Fall. Once again, my trust in God's ways grew as He revealed His faithfulness.

After Michael had finished his own prayer time, he came to me and said, "God told me Pastor Phillipe is definitely the Pastor of the church."

"What? Are you sure Michael?"

With a stern gaze, he said, "Of course, Amy! Aren't you excited?!"

220

"Oh hon, that's perfect!" I ran over and embraced him tightly, relieved at God's unexpected answer.

"Yes, and he said selection of elders and deacons was to commence immediately. He also clearly told me that our role was over now."

Surprised, I said again, "Michael, are you sure?"

"Yes, I know we thought our time would end next year. But God told me as clear as a bell that we are done here as soon as everything is finished. And you know what that means, we need to obey His will and leave."

"You're completely certain?"

"Yes, absolutely," Michael responded.

"And I am not going to be disobedient like we were for the many years before we actually came on mission. We need to figure out where we are moving, Amy."

Michael's certainty confirmed what I thought the Holy Spirit had been telling me as well; now I was thankful we agreed. For months I had been awaiting God's final call of leadership, thinking Michael and I would oversee the installation and formalities of the bylaws and constitution for the church, but God's plan was otherwise.

Over the next week, after we continued to pray together seeking clarity about this decision, Michael and I learned from the Holy Spirit that we had done exactly as the Lord had asked and been faithful to our call. Our mission was complete; we needed to leave. The Discipleship House would be the last piece of His church building. God was very clear this was to be a church for the Haitian community and the "white people" as they called us, were not to be in leadership.

The Holy Spirit even went further to let us know if we did stay, we would be enabling the people not to lead, as this is the role we had since the ministry's movement into Blackwood. "It is over," God said. He could handle the installation of the formalities of organizing the church. He was God Almighty and could take it from here.

We knew it was important to coordinate the church plant through our local church in the Bahamas. Even though some in the leadership had not experienced a heart transformation of abiding by love in Christ versus strict adherence to works, we still believed in the local church and the mandate of being a church for the city. We were living out the Apostle Paul's words from Acts 14:20–21, 23, "... he rose up and entered the city... preached the gospel to that city and had made many disciples. And when they had appointed elders for them...they committed them to the Lord in whom they believed."

Our local leadership had already participated in this church plant, agreeing to oversee the Haitian church formalities. There was the confirmation and approval of Haitian leadership and implementation of the church bylaws and constitution as well. Their partnership was God's will for His church within this city and we prayed He could use this plan to show others how the power of the gospel of grace changes lives and brings forth a believer's righteousness and justification.

God was clearly working; the Haitian church was to be an extension of the local Bahamian church and thus God's plan would triumph in bringing unity to a culture that had been separated by deep ethnocentrism for years. What a victory! The Peoples Church in the Bahamas would be helping the Haitian church in Blackwood. They didn't have a name yet until the Pastor selected it, but we called it *The Gathering*.

For the first time in months, God's will for His church and our family was clear and precise, resulting in amazing peace. Although we loved our life and could not fathom leaving, we knew our journey reflected that of the Apostle Paul in the book of Acts. Paul moved on after he planted churches like the one in Ephesus. This revelation gave us tremendous strength and courage. Just as Paul loved his brethren dearly, we did too, but now we needed to leave for much needed refreshment. When I heard the Holy Spirit say, *Rest and refuge, Amy,* relief washed over me. Throughout this journey, we knew we would not want to be disobedient to God ever again as we did when we made the commitment to come to the Bahamas the first time.

Michael and I fasted and prayed about a new beginning. *Where?* Once again became the question since the *when* was determined.

As the summer 2016 mission teams finished, we were excited to see this church, which included the main sanctuary and a separate building for discipleship, would indeed bring unity and stability to the community.

Under God's directive, we were grateful to have been used as stewards of His work. Being available for Jesus we followed his plan and created multiple ministries within Blackwood. What God had begun with a simple directive of *Move to the Bahamas* had blossomed from the unknown, to His name being known and His glory being unleashed.

As Pastor Phillipe and the Haitian Blackwood community held a farewell service for our family late in July, we cried tears of joy. I prayed, *Oh Lord I am thankful for Pastor Phillipe, but you know my heart. We are missing the leadership that is needed! Please provide. I believe we both know who I am speaking about Lord so open this door! Please open his heart to embrace his calling.*

We still had a few more pieces that needed to fall into place.

The Last Supper – Saying Goodbye

And I saw the holy city, new Jerusalem, coming down out of heaven from God, prepared as a bride adorned for her husband.

Revelation 21:2

After our precious Haitian friends threw us a farewell party as a proper send off at church, we also had our own good-bye party for those who we were closest to us in ministry. That Thursday night in July before our departure the next day, I stood on the porch of the mission house, tears gently cascading down my cheeks as I looked at my last Bahama sunset. One by one I watched the beloved Haitian young men and women take their chair from the dinner table and bring it to the other end of the porch and form a circle. I turned my chair from watching the sunset and joined them in the circle. Night was descending, and Michael opened in prayer.

He shared the intimate thoughts of his heart with our core discipleship group. I followed him saying, "Everyone, please know how grateful we are for allowing us the honor to be a part of your lives and to be a part of your journey as followers of Jesus."

I then turned intently towards Davidson, shutting my eyes for a moment and praying silently, *Please Lord, I pray Davidson will be bold and accept your invitation like we did in faith.*

As I raised my eyes, I caught his gaze and said, "Davidson you know Mr. Michael and I love you so much. You know since the moment I laid eyes on you on that bicycle in the corner of the field you captured my heart and I knew God had big plans for you. I want you to remember all that Mr. Michael and I have spoken to you about. You know we have told you our desire is that you disciple these younger boys here and rise to the leadership position we believe God is wanting for you."

By this point Davidson had bowed his head and had his hands clasped as if in prayer. I knew from this posture he was still vacillating about taking on this role permanently. Michael and I clearly felt Davidson needed to be the full-time youth pastor with the new Church. He had helped facilitate the teams over the years with the ministry and led some of the younger boys in the discipleship group but now he needed to choose working part time in ministry or committing his full life to the Lord working for the church. Michael and I had prayed for Davidson to step out in faith and surrender to the life in ministry which we believed God was asking of him. Now would finally be his opportunity to be "all in" for Jesus.

Slowly he lifted his head up and looked at me. Finally, he said, "Yes, Ms. Amy, I know you are right. I am in. I will lead the boys and be the Youth Pastor. I already met with Pastor Phillipe."

Relief washed over me, and I immediately stood up and embraced him and thanked him. I knew this was the final puzzle piece for me. My prayer was answered, and God again was victorious. As we joined hands for our final prayer, I laid my hands directly on Davidson and prayed with abandon that God would equip him to know that "...faith is the assurance of things hoped for, the conviction of things not seen" as stated in Hebrews 11:1. This command would be the key to following Jesus for Davidson as it was for my family and me.

With Davidson and Pastor Phillipe in leadership the Blackwood church was left in good hands. The official name of the church was instituted by the locals now and changed from what the ministry had called it to the "New Jerusalem Church." The name came about after one of the women in the Bible study, who was a close friend of mine, relayed a remarkable dream that she had to Pastor Phillipe. In that dream she said God told her the church name was to be "New Jerusalem Church." This name would signify they were Jesus' bride, adorned and ready for the coming King.

Although it was incredibly difficult that next morning to leave the life God had blessed us with over the course of six years, we were certain we'd be coming back. All along we believed we would be returning to the Bahamas to facilitate teams over the following year and help the church transition. Taking only seven bags to the dock that morning, we left a garage full of ministry supplies and food and other personal belongings like Christmas ornaments and winter clothes to use in the upcoming months when we met teams.

The next morning when we arrived at the dock to catch our ferry, we were surprised to see a small group of our closest Bahamian friends waiting for our arrival. With tearful hugs we said our good-bye's thinking in three short months we would be reunited.

But a month after we arrived in the US, the Holy Spirit had Michael and I fast and pray for two days and we learned that we would not return to our beloved sojourners until God told us to go back.

Here we were again, surrendered to God and in the same situation we had begun our journey with him on-clinging to God by faith, trusting Him to show us how to start a new life all over again in the USA.

As God always does, this news coincided with an amazing report from New Jerusalem Church. Pastor Phillipe sent video, pictures and a report two weeks after our departure that the attendance at the church services was well over seventy members and five persons had professed belief and repentance in Jesus.

Home Again

As of summer's end in 2018 the church has tripled in size and has already expanded twice since our departure in July of 2016. The Bible studies continue seamlessly with leaders overseeing the younger adults and astonishingly, God has brought others alongside his church to preach, teach and encourage the Haitians.

Also, within months of our leaving, amazingly the Bahamian pastor from another nearby Methodist church taught alongside his Haitian pilgrims with Davidson translating for him from English into Creole. After the service he gave a five-hundred-dollar donation to them as a sign of love and comradery in Christ.

* * * * * * *

Today I can reflect on how blessed my family and I have been by the life God gifted us with in the Bahamas. I am overwhelmed as I recollect all He did in six short years. We have a group of lasting friendships that are grounded in Christ from the nations. Our family is overcome with gratefulness for the close bonds to local Bahamians, Haitian brothers and sisters and many different people from all over the United States.

God has allowed our family to be a small part of many people's lives and spiritual growth and in turn they too have poured into our spiritual growth. With many confessions of faith and baptisms from US team participants as well as Blackwood kids and young adults, we have been able to watch people come to repentance and belief. We've also had the privilege of participating in their learning and growing in faith and become a part of a universal church of followers of Jesus. We maintain close ties to many of these same participants via phone conversations and email throughout the year. These friendships have been able to grow, and discipleship is occurring on multiple levels going beyond islands and oceans!

In June of 2018, Pastor Phillipe accompanied seventeen members of his congregation back to their home country of Haiti to hold a crusade for Christ. Miraculously many Haitian brothers and sisters accepted Jesus for the first time by repentance and belief.

Today, Suze is still flourishing in Haiti and praying about God's call on her life and a ministry for her own people sharing Jesus Christ and the transforming hope of His gospel. She is passionate about showing Christ's love and is working with other locals ministering to her fellow Haitians. Our family has gone to Haiti several times helping her make disciples and mentor others and are praying about how we can help Suze with the details of what God wants, seeking His wisdom as to how it will unfold. Even after consistent denial for a Visa to the Bahamas, God opened the door for her to obtain a US Visa. Now she is able to spend time with us, her family, in the USA and will continue to travel with us in the future.

It has only been by the Holy Spirit that we have been changed from reflecting an American portrait of success to being God's image bearers. My family and I are a true testament to the power of God's word. It has transformed our family's heart, mind and soul. It has molded and shaped us and taught us all about living our lives centered on Jesus.

I was in love with the *idea* of Jesus before I followed His command and obeyed His challenge to forsake all I had for Him alone. Now I love Jesus. He is my King; the Author and Perfecter of my faith; my Everything. He revealed that my best efforts and best plans could never surpass the Way he has laid out for me and my family today. Every inch of my being is immersed in yearning for Him and wanting to pursue His glory so that others can taste and see the amazing love Jesus offers.

Still Letting Go

The process of surrender has not been easy; many times, it's been painful, but Jesus tells us in Matthew 11:29 to 30, "Take my yoke upon you, and learn from me, for I am meek and lowly in heart, and you will find rest to your souls. For my yoke is easy, and my burden is light." God's success looks different from the world's ideas of success, amassing money and worshipping other idols of title, status and wealth to give one identity or security. But no words can adequately express the blessed joy of following Jesus. A life abiding with Him is true abundance. Paul says in Galatians

2:20, "I have been crucified with Christ. and it is no longer I who live, but Christ who lives in me; and the life which I now live in the flesh I live by faith in the Son of God, who loved me and gave Himself up for me."

A Challenge to You, Beloved

As I look back on this journey of faith, I want to encourage anyone who would call themselves a Christian to examine their hearts and see if they are missing something. Is there a heartfelt satisfaction missing because you are not living a life for the only One who satisfies? Do you feel divided about the focus in your mind and your interests?

Consider this: Is the overriding urge within your soul for Christ to be at the center of everything you do and say in *all* areas of your life? Do you know that Christ's nature is within you and that any bad habit can be masterfully changed by clinging to the very nature He has bestowed on you as a believer? Can you understand that what might seem like an impossibility or problem in your life is God's opportunity? That you as a believer can receive the promises in the Bible and the power of the Holy Spirit to overcome difficulties while growing in faith and becoming more Christ-like? Beloved, the journey of faith is the Way to develop you as God already sees you in Christ.

This Way is the blessing of the "abundant life." It is a heart that is constantly looking to Jesus in word and prayer. It is a heart that constantly yields to the gift of the Holy Spirit. It is a whole person totally and completely focused on surrendering all that He has and all that he is to the One who gives beyond our wildest imagination.

We are being called to a banquet laid out for all who are willing to come. To partake in the feast and experience God's Way does not look like what the world teaches but is far better than our grandest expectations. It is about sacrificial love that is carried out in all that you do, think and say.

The power of God's love is like the words from the children's song, "Magic Penny." The chorus is a great demonstration of reciprocal love: "Love is something if you give it away, give it away, give it away. Love is something if you give away, you end up having more."

When you as a follower of Jesus give the very love, He implants within you, namely Himself, you take this love to others and show the magnitude of this Wonderful Jesus. By doing so, you are used to point others to Him. In my own life when I do this, the blessing I receive back is 100 times more than I ever gave away.

Scripture tells us in 2 John 6 to "walk in love." Our lives are to be so filled with the God whose name is love from 1 John 4:8 that we are to instinctively live everyday life with Him at the center of our soul. The blessing is that in return as we give away, He gives it back, but He gets the glory! We are the conduit for His glory and being used as such becomes an honor and privilege.

My story is still in the making, but I am thankful for the gift of being used in one small area of the world for God's glory. I pray you can see that God chooses His mission for each of us and it is for His names' sake. God can teach you and transform you by the Holy Spirit if you allow yourself to yield to Him. If you are willing, He will exceed any earthly dream you aspire towards.

Ask God what His plan is for you

What will you do in your sphere of influence to build His kingdom? The choice is yours, but you must be willing to die...die to manmade dreams, manmade ideas, manmade knowledge and focus on the Lord of the Universe, our eternal King who can indeed supply all you need for this life and the life to come! I can testify wholeheartedly to the truth in Philippians 1:21, "For to me to live is Christ and to die is gain."

Ultimately, that dying to what I thought my life would look like and surrendering to the Holy Spirit's beckoning to follow was the pivotal decision I made in my life: would I pursue God's Way or my own way? My life truly began when I surrendered to a journey of faith. I learned participating at the wedding feast with Christ began that day but will continue throughout my lifetime by living faith. I learned that the hole within me will never be satisfied until I am adorned as the bride of the church in my entire splendor with Christ as my groom in His everlasting kingdom.

Michael, my earthly husband, will never fulfill me nor was he ever meant to meet this role. It is only through our mutual sanctification in Christ's redeeming love that we can assure our earthly call to marriage. We do this by remaining in our covenant commitment of love despite our daily disappointments of bad habits; this commitment to walk through challenges is what yields our sanctification. Ultimately showing Jesus' mysterious splendor and majesty are only exhibited in the gospel of grace. This holiness defines me and fulfills me not only in my marriage but in who I am and in all I do. Jesus answered my question of surrender and showed me that I will never be truly satisfied until I join Him in eternity.

For now, my life's mission is to come to the feast proclaiming, "Not to us, O LORD, but to your name give glory, for the sake of your steadfast love and your faithfulness!" As Psalm 115:1 says. By living out "He must increase, but I must decrease," as found in John 3:30, He alone fills me and allows my cup to run over. It is this love in my heart that allows me to show the same to others.

Coming to the feast is the first step but remaining at the table is the journey.

Today, I could not imagine a life other than living by faith. I am grateful to God for placing me and my family in that same position all over again when we returned to the States to settle in Florida. By doing so, He has shown me He alone is in control and the life of abiding by faith gives an intimacy of knowing the triune God in its fullness. The Words of Jesus best describe this fullness and presence in John 17: 26, "I made known to them your name, and I will continue to make it known, that the love with which you have loved me may be in them, and I in them."

Dwelling with Christ can be described as coming to His feast. It is constant rejoicing and celebration not dependent on your circumstances. It is joy that surpasses your comprehension. It is this Way, "*the* Way," which is a glass overflowing, baskets abounding with bread, a rainbow times ten, and a birthday party that you wake up to every day.

Listen for Him, ask Him and as He beckons you to His banquet, pick up your cross, I mean fork, and come feast on the only food that can satisfy, the wedding feast of Jesus Christ!

ACKNOWLEDGMENTS

Completing an impossible task that God has put on your heart can only be accomplished with the many parts of the body of Christ lending a hand.

Without other followers coming alongside us, our story would never been accomplished to fulfill God's intended will. Writing "The Way" has been such a journey and I have many people to thank.

First and foremost, I want to thank my amazing husband, Michael who has faithfully stood by my side loving me every step of the Way. Our beautiful children: Luke, Marley, Josie, James and Suzelynda had no other choice but to live this narrow road with Michael and I and without their cooperation we would have never accomplished building God's kingdom. Thank you. I love you more than words can express.

I also want to thank our personal families, the many US mission teams, donors, churches and Fellowship of Christian Athletes. Finally, no book is written alone, and I cannot thank my talented Editor, Jody Lee Collins, and book designer, William Johnson enough.

Lastly, Michael and I are grateful to the people of Spanish Wells and The People's Church of the Bahamas. We adore and thank our beloved sojourners, the Haitian people of the neighborhoods of Apea and Blackwood who welcomed us in with open hearts.

"Now to the King eternal, immortal, invisible, the only God, be honor and glory forever and ever. Amen." 1 Timothy 1:17

By Faith In Jesus,

Amy Boykin
Destin, Florida

April 2019

Made in the USA
Columbia, SC
12 May 2022